EDMONTON
BENEATH OUR FEET

EDMONTON
BENEATH OUR FEET

A guide to the
geology of the
Edmonton region

John D. Godfrey
Editor-in-Chief

Edmonton Geological Society

The Publisher:
Edmonton Geological Society

Canadian Cataloguing-in-Publication Data
Edmonton Geological Society
1. Edmonton Beneath Our Feet
2. A Guide to the Geology of the Edmonton Region
   ISBN 0-9697107-0-4

Book and cover design: R. Dale Hite
Production by:
Hite Graphic Services Ltd.
1170-68 Street
Edmonton, Alberta T6K 3K4

Front cover photograph:
Badlands landscape in Dawson Park, Edmonton, Raymond McDonald
Back cover photograph: John D. Godfrey

Graphics: Dan Magee and Jim Matthie
Sketches: Geoffrey Lester, Michael Fisher
Printing : Quality Color Press Inc.

Edmonton Geological Society Publication Committee:
E.W. Brooker, P. Erdmer, J.D. Godfrey, B. Hitchon, C.W. Langenberg

SPONSORS

The production of this book was supported through donations by the following organizations and individuals:

■ $1,000 to 10,000

Canadian Geological Foundation
Canadian Society of Petroleum
  Geologists
Economic Development Edmonton
Edmonton Community Foundation
Alberta Research Council
Interprovincial Pipe Line Inc.
IOF Foresters

■ $250 to 1,000

Chieftain International, Inc.
Nova Corporation of Alberta
Whitmore Development Corp.
Inland Cement Limited
Northwestern Utilities
Edmonton Power
UMA Engineering Ltd.
EBA Engineering Consultants Ltd.
PCL Construction Group Inc.
Wells Construction Ltd.
T.B.G. Contracting Ltd.
L.W. Nelson

■ $100 to 250

Numac Oil and Gas Ltd.
Thurber Management
Carousel Photographics
L. Dunn
B. Bennett
G. McCormick
G. Cuddy
Garrity & Baker Drilling (1979) Ltd.
Mobile Augers
N. Morgenstern
H. Rix
P. Evans
A.D. Williams Engineering
An-Geo Environmental Consultants
Wigham Resources Ltd.
D. Lindberg
HBT Agra Ltd.
The City of Edmonton
S. Blazenko
Godfrey Tours
P. Erdmer
D. Cruden
D. Wightman
W. Langenberg
H. Charlesworth
H. Machel
M. Dufresne
Hitchon Geochemical Services
R. Folinsbee
R. Strobl
Alberta Chamber of Resources
N.W. Woywitka
J.G. Wright
S.A. Antoniuk
J.W. Kramers
G.W. Bernard
Bedrock Supply
W.J. Sanderson
D.E. Mills
G.D. Mossop

CONTENTS

PREFACE

The aim of this book is to present geological information about the Edmonton region in a form useful to geologists and engineers and yet understandable by a broad segment of the interested public. This book serves as a source of practical and scientific information about the geological foundations of our city, and as a convenient field guide to exploring and understanding the landscapes which form the backdrop to everyday life in much of central Alberta. The Edmonton Geological Society wishes you many interesting hours of exploring Edmonton beneath your feet.

Edmonton, Alberta
March 1993

ACKNOWLEDGMENTS

In the Fall of 1991, the Edmonton Geological Society decided to publish a book on the geology of Edmonton for the May 1993 annual conference of the Geological Association of Canada, to be held in Edmonton. At the request of the Society, Dr. John D. Godfrey became the book's editor-in-chief, and he gave freely of his time throughout the two-year undertaking. He managed all practical aspects of the production. Dr. Godfrey was joined by Dr. Elmer W. Brooker in a successful fund-raising effort to meet the cost of publishing the book in its present attractive format. Without the dedication of these two individuals, the project would not have been completed. The Society gratefully acknowledges their essential contribution. In addition, all authors, who volunteered contributions to this book, are thanked for their efforts.

The majority of these authors are affiliated with major institutions in Edmonton – The University of Alberta, Alberta Research Council, The Alberta Provincial Museum – which are sincerely thanked for their support of this project.

1 INTRODUCTION

John D. Godfrey

The foundations of our modern and increasingly industrialized society have come to rely more and more on a wide variety of raw materials taken from the Earth. Consequently, geology, the science that studies the Earth, touches each one of us, numerous times, every day, in a multitude of ways and on a wide range of scales. The Earth provides the raw materials from which familiar things are produced. The degree of sophistication used in manufacturing technology has evolved through time. The Romans made concrete foundations, clay bricks and roofing tiles, tools and weapons of steel, ceramic vessels for the household, and so on. These same raw materials are used today as in the past. Only the technology has changed, a little in some cases and a great deal in others.

Not only do we place heavy reliance on natural resources as the ingredients of our material goods, but we also use the fuels that ancient rocks so generously provide with which to manufacture them – coal, oil, natural gas, oil sands and uranium. All of these raw materials, the fuels and the non-fuels, are present in limited economic quantities. They are non-renewable resources, for which we must accept custodianship.

The wise use of these limited resources is concerned not only with efficient conservation measures, but also with the side effects of that usage, the production of waste end-products (gases, liquids and solids) that are now recognized for their largely negative impact on the natural environment. That negative impact is identified as a real threat to all life on Earth and now calls for serious assessments and counter-measures to be undertaken by all interested and involved parties.

The use of raw materials from the Earth has allowed us to create comfortable lifestyles, to inhabit hitherto hostile environments, and to support and sustain a healthy well-being for many civilizations over time around the world.

Studies in geology have shed light on the origin and history of planet Earth and on the nature of the continents and the surrounding oceans. Geology provides insight into the origin and evolution of landscapes and seascapes, and allows us to conjecture about the impact of processes on environments that will continue to affect our daily lives far into the future.

The preservation of life forms in the fossil record has given us a unique opportunity to seek and to see the evolutionary connections through geological time. The diversification of life has progressively become more complex, spreading from the ocean basins onto land, thereby occupying every possible ecological niche. The use of radioactive minerals has enabled geologists to measure the age of rocks and to give an estimate of the great antiquity of the Earth – our home planet. The span of the fourth dimension of time has a special meaning for geologists and constitutes a humbling concept for most of us. A routine daily journey in Edmonton can take us across a scenic valley that did not exist 12,000 years ago. Sedimentary layers exposed in the lower slopes of that valley were laid down more than 65 million years ago, and granite boulders, brought into the area by glaciers some 20,000 years ago and now lying in the river bed, date back to almost 2000 million years ago. Yet, perhaps the greatest contribution that the science of geology has made to the body of our general knowledge is a plausible measurement of the time of birth of planet Earth, some 4600 million years in the past.

Engineers constantly apply geology and interrelate with geologists as together they endeavor to meet daily challenges through their special knowledge and use of earth materials.

Adverse ground conditions are monitored and solutions are generated to resolve problems that may concern habitation, travel or the support systems for our accepted standards of safe living. The effective operation of settlements requires a largely hidden lattice-work of structures and services beneath the urban landscape in order to make them function reliably. When systems overload and fail, solutions need to be engineered quickly to overcome the immediate crises. The complex vital nerve system of a city includes such things as: a supply of consistently clean, safe water, an efficient road network and public transportation, telecommunications, solid waste disposal, a 24-hour supply of energy sources, and adequate waste and storm sewer capacity for the safety, comfort and convenience of its citizens.

It is hoped that this book will enable the reader to understand better the complex and interesting history of this part of Alberta, as well as to appreciate the work of countless geologists in unravelling this history. Not the least, the reader should go away with the knowledge of how geology impacts profoundly on our daily life.

2 THE EDMONTON REGION THROUGH TIME

Geology

Roger D. Morton

■ Geological History

The geology of the Edmonton region reveals a fascinating story of some 2000 million years of our continent's history, a substantial portion of the Earth's total age of 4600 million years (Figure 1). As the pages of the local geological record are unfolded, we discover evidence of constantly changing landscapes, climates, faunas and floras in what is presently called Western Canada. To understand the reasons for such dramatic changes it is essential to fully appreciate the fact that the Earth is not static but is a dynamic entity, driven both by internal and by external forces. An internal heat engine within the Earth's hot interior stirs its mantle and causes movement of crustal plates across the surface. The energy imparted to the atmosphere and hydrosphere by the Sun's radiation drives the hydrological cycle and the weather systems. These in turn govern the rates and varieties of physical and chemical weathering of rocks, the transport of their breakdown products and the nature of the sediments ultimately deposited.

Continental mountain ranges such as the Rocky Mountains of western Alberta normally form when continental and oceanic plates collide or when two continents collide. The immense force of such collisions can compress the Earth's crust into great folded mountain belts and rip apart the crust along enormous fault surfaces.

The City of Edmonton is situated upon a succession of strata deposited by various geological processes over the buried margin of the ancient Precambrian basement of North America (the so-called Canadian Shield). Over millions of years, forces of erosion wore down the rocks both of the Canadian Shield to the north and of the Cordillera to the west. Thus, most of Alberta is underlain by a 2 to 3 km thick blanket of erosional debris which has been converted during burial into a series of clastic sedimentary rocks such as conglomerates, sandstones and shales. Before the Rocky Mountains were built up, the Pacific Ocean occasionally flooded into this region. Thus, marine sedimentary rocks such as limestone and dolostone also make up a significant portion of the stratigraphic succession beneath Alberta.

The prehistory of the Edmonton region is preserved in various chapters of the geological record and each is examined in turn below. In order to follow the details of the story, one must appreciate some of the fundamental processes in the building of the geological

3

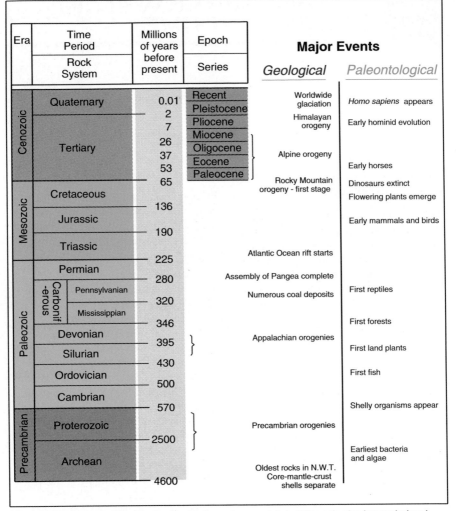

Era	Time Period / Rock System	Millions of years before present	Epoch / Series	Major Events	
				Geological	Paleontological
Cenozoic	Quaternary	0.01	Recent	Worldwide glaciation	Homo sapiens appears
		2	Pleistocene		
		7	Pliocene	Himalayan orogeny	Early hominid evolution
	Tertiary	26	Miocene		
		37	Oligocene	Alpine orogeny	
		53	Eocene		Early horses
		65	Paleocene	Rocky Mountain orogeny - first stage	Dinosaurs extinct
Mesozoic	Cretaceous				Flowering plants emerge
		136			
	Jurassic				Early mammals and birds
		190			
	Triassic			Atlantic Ocean rift starts	
		225			
Paleozoic	Permian			Assembly of Pangea complete	
		280			
	Carboniferous — Pennsylvanian			Numerous coal deposits	First reptiles
		320			
	Carboniferous — Mississippian				First forests
		346			
	Devonian			Appalachian orogenies	First land plants
		395			
	Silurian				
		430			First fish
	Ordovician				
		500			
	Cambrian				Shelly organisms appear
		570			
Precambrian	Proterozoic			Precambrian orogenies	
		2500			Earliest bacteria and algae
	Archean			Oldest rocks in N.W.T. Core-mantle-crust shells separate	
		4600			

Figure 1. The Geological Time Scale, showing the major mountain-building episodes (orogenies) and milestones of biological evolution in the fossil record.

framework of Western Canada. We will see how the Canadian Shield became the nucleus around which the continent grew larger, and how millennia of erosion and deposition draped the margin of the Shield with blankets of sediments. Some 150 million years ago, the mobile crustal floor of the Pacific Ocean began to collide with the North American continental plate. The result was to compress and fold the previously deposited sedimentary blanket, thereby forming the Western Cordillera and the Rocky Mountain belt.

Much of the geological history of Alberta as understood today is founded upon the pioneering efforts of earlier geologists. This is especially true of the work of J.A. Allan, first head and founder of the Department of Geology at the University of Alberta.

■ Precambrian Basement – the opening chapter

(Time zero to 2500 million years ago)

The ancient rocks of the Precambrian basement, a buried extension of the Canadian Shield, lie beneath 2 km of younger rocks in the Edmonton district. To actually see and walk on the ancient nucleus of the North American continent we can travel to the northeast corner of Alberta, around Lake Athabasca at Fort Chipewyan. There, the great continental glaciers of Quaternary time and earlier phases of erosion have ripped deep into the crust, stripped off the younger strata and revealed the ancient rocks below. The depth to the Precambrian rocks of the basement is known from many localities in Alberta where deep oil wells have penetrated through the sedimentary cover (Figure 2).

Wherever the Precambrian basement of Alberta has been observed it is composed of metamorphic and igneous rocks. Such rock types attest to their formation under high temperatures and pressures of the same magnitude as exist deep below mountain ranges today. Thus, we deduce that the Shield below Alberta largely represents the eroded roots of an ancient Precambrian mountain chain.

John Andrew Allan (1884-1955)

John Allan, Alberta's first resident geologist, founded the Geology Department at the University of Alberta and was an original member of the Alberta Research Council. Allan was born in Aubrey, Quebec and educated at McGill University and the Massachusetts Institute of Technology. Allan came to the West as an assistant with the Geological Survey of Canada and many of his early studies were on the Rocky Mountains, including the rare igneous rocks of the Ice River Alkaline Complex near Field, B.C.. In 1912, Allan was appointed to the University of Alberta, where he initiated the teaching of geology and practiced it with great skill and enthusiasm for the next forty years. John Allan considered himself Professor of the University, not just of geology. As such he was concerned about the overall well-being of his students. He wanted to give them a whole education, which included English and Ethics.

In 1920 the Alberta Government established the Scientific and Industrial Research Council of Alberta (now the Alberta Research Council) to ascertain the mineral resources of the province and their possibilities for development. Allan directed the Geology Section of the Council from within the university for twenty nine years. His wide-ranging interests and great versatility led him to publish on all aspects of economic geology including coal, salt deposits, and the relations of geology to soils. In 1926 Allan produced the first geological map of the province and in 1927 helped found the Canadian Society of Petroleum Geologists. Allan was interested in all aspects of education and worked very hard to build the Geology Museum at the university.

Allan loved the Rocky Mountains, was a strong climber and spent most of his holidays there. He was in great physical. It is very fitting that a mountain was named after him. Mt. Allan became well known as a ski-venue during the 1988 Calgary Winter Olympics.

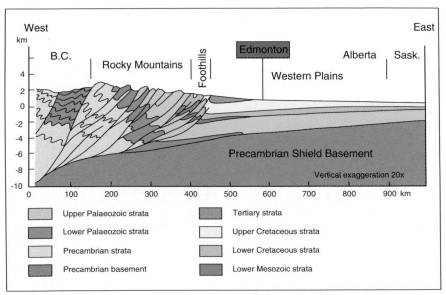

Figure 2. Simplified schematic (vertically exaggerated) cross-section extending west - east from the Rocky Mountains through the foothills and plains of Western Canada.

The ages of these Precambrian rocks have been determined (using isotope analysis) by geochronologists working at the University of Alberta. The geochronological studies reveal that the original sedimentary and volcanic rocks of the Alberta basement were laid down some 3500 to 2500 million years ago. These rocks were later metamorphosed and in part melted during the period 2300 to 1700 million years ago when they were deformed during the collision of primitive continental and oceanic crustal plates. Thus, these deformed rocks were forced down into the lower crust, 10 to 20 km below surface, where temperatures reached 400° to 600°C. At such high temperatures and pressures, most rocks recrystallize and even partially melt to form magmas.

Thus, the Precambrian rocks of Alberta's basement became

transformed (metamorphosed) from their original states into schists and gneisses. Such metamorphosed rocks look very different from their original sedimentary and volcanic precursors, for their minerals have been largely re-organized. This is a great pity because metamorphism also destroyed the physical traces of primitive, soft-bodied life forms, such as cyanobacteria (blue-green algae) which developed in oceans and rivers at least 3500 million years ago. These bacteria, like modern plants, could photosynthesize organic chemicals and give off oxygen. They were responsible for the primitive anoxic atmosphere becoming oxygenated and capable of supporting most of the life forms we know today.

Although outcrops of the Precambrian Shield are not available around Edmonton, samples of similar metamorphic/igneous Precambrian basement rocks are to be seen at many places in the region. Nature has been kind enough to transport these rocks and man has arranged them in attractive fieldstone walls and fireplaces around Edmonton. Many of the gravel pits and fields around the City expose Pleistocene tills. These tills represent the debris dumped by continental glaciers which swept into the area from the northeast. The tills contain boulders and pebbles of Precambrian Shield rocks preserved in them. Many of the larger boulders (erratics) in the tills have been collected and displayed in gardens and parks around the City. Boulders of pink or red granite and black and white striped gneiss have undeniable aesthetic appeal in landscape design. A variety of erratic boulders in Rundle Park is listed in Chapter 5 (Site 9).

■ Proterozoic Eon – the destruction of mountain ranges

(2500 to 570 million years ago)

The series of crustal plate collisions (termed Plate Tectonics) which formed the mountains of the western Shield ceased around 1750 million years ago. Continental uplift and renewed river erosion contrived to wear away the Precambrian mountains. At first, the relief on the Shield would have been dramatic and thick aprons of coarse clastic detritus would be shed from the mountains and carried westward by rivers toward the sea. These blankets of

ancient gravels and sands are preserved in part as the sandstones and conglomerates of the Proterozoic Athabasca Group in the northeast corner of Alberta, around Lake Athabasca. Most of the Proterozoic clastic strata were removed by later erosion and do not, therefore, occur in other parts of the Province.

It is in the remnant patch of Athabasca Group strata that vast deposits of rich uranium ore were discovered in the period 1970 to 1980. Although Alberta does not have an active uranium mine, neighbouring Saskatchewan produces a large portion of the Western World's current nuclear raw material from Athabasca Group rocks.

But what of the regions farther away from the Shield, e.g. in western Alberta? It was there that the river-borne debris from the Shield mountains was being dumped into the sea. Thus, if we travel to the Jasper, Banff or Waterton Lakes national parks, we find Proterozoic strata 1100 to 570 million years old which were laid down under marine conditions far from the Shield. Here, finer-grained sandstones and shales are interbedded with limestones and thick turbidites. Such turbidites were the products of dense gravel-sand-mudflows which roared through submarine canyons into the deeper reaches of the Proterozoic sea. It is probable that such Proterozoic sediments once underlay Edmonton, but they were subsequently eroded during the Paleozoic Era.

Younger Proterozoic rocks in Alberta have been typically only mildly affected by metamorphism. These strata were never deeply buried in the crust, having been only touched by the relatively low temperatures and low pressures of the shallower parts of the Rocky Mountain Orogeny.

■ Paleozoic Era
– a tropical paradise in Alberta

(570 to 245 million years ago)

Strata of Paleozoic age have played a profound role in the economic development of Alberta and Western Canada. It is these strata which have supplied a wealth of industrial minerals, oil and natural gas.

During the Paleozoic Era, Alberta basked under the tropical sun between latitudes 30° North and 30° South (Figure 3). The Province had been carried there, probably in Cambrian time, by the drifting of the North American plate.

As the Paleozoic Era dawned in Western Canada, there was no profound and obvious change in the landscape. The old Precambrian mountains of the Shield were still being worn down and sands, silts and clays were transported by rivers to the shore of the Pacific Ocean. The changes which were about to take place in the biosphere were, however, quite profound. These seas had already been the site of some major evolutionary changes in animal life forms for some time. In late Proterozoic time some well-organized, soft-bodied animals inhabited the well-lit seas of the old Pacific coast. At the dawn of the Paleozoic Era the seas, already populated by these sophisticated

Percival Sidney Warren (1890-1970)

P.S. Warren was the first stratigrapher and palaeontologist at the University of Alberta. Warren was born at Brechin, Ontario and educated at the University of Toronto. His thesis work was on the stratigraphy and paleontology of the Banff area, published as the classic 1927 Memoir 153 of the Geological Survey of Canada, "the Banff memoir".

Warren joined the staff of the University of Alberta in 1920 and remained active there until his death in 1970, a half century later. Warren, J.A. Allan and R.L. Rutherford formed a triumvirate which was the strength of geological research and teaching at the University of Alberta for thirty years.

Warren was active with the Research Council of Alberta, authoring many of the palaeontology sections of their numerous field reports, often in collaboration with J.A. Allan and R.L. Rutherford. In addition, Warren was often associated with the Geological Survey of Canada, leading and assisting a variety of their field parties. Warren collected and published extensively on the Paleozoic and Mesozoic rocks of western and northern Canada, building the extensive biostratigraphic collection at the University of Alberta. Warren and his collections were frequently consulted during the height of oil exploration following World War II.

Although Professor Warren received many honours during his career, the most treasured was having the student geological society at the University of Alberta named after him.

soft-bodied organisms, were gradually colonized by hard-shelled organisms such as trilobites.

Early Devonian(400 million years ago)
Tropical climate

Late Devonian(360 million years ago)
Tropical climate

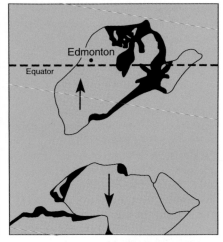

Pennsylvanian(300 million years ago)
Sub-tropical climate

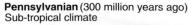

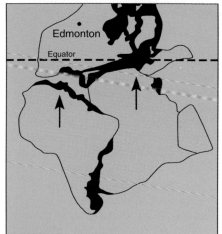

Early Cretaceous(120 million years ago)
Warm temperate to Mediterranean climate

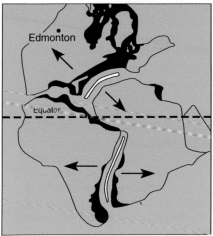

Figure 3. Plate movement and the changing
climate of Western Canada from 400 to 120 million
years ago.

In Alberta the oldest Cambrian strata are known as the Gog Group. These rocks are exposed in the front ranges of the Rocky Mountains in Jasper National Park (e.g. at Pyramid Mountain) but are not present beneath Edmonton. However, samples of these Lower Cambrian rocks are widespread around Edmonton. Virtually every hard, rounded, buff or white pebble that we see in the North Saskatchewan River valley is a sample of Lower Cambrian Gog Group quartzite. This quartzite was formed from a white sand which accumulated along the shoreline of the Cambrian sea. It was later metamorphosed during the Cordilleran mountain-building event, and transformed from a quartz-rich sandstone into the hard, resistant quartzite we see today. These quartzites were extensively used by the aboriginal North American Indian population of Alberta to produce utilitarian tools such as scrapers, spears and arrowheads (see Wright, Chapter 2.).

For much of Cambrian time and at least until early Ordovician time (i.e. between 570 and 438 million years ago), Alberta was covered by a tropical sea, rather like the modern Caribbean Sea. Under such conditions marine life flourished and the ocean floors were covered by thick deposits of calcium carbonate mud. This limy mud ultimately became limestone.

The climate was so hot that shallow waters and lagoons evaporated to produce salt deposits and warm magnesium-rich brines, just as in the modern Red Sea region. These brines reacted with the calcium carbonate muds to produce the mineral dolomite (calcium magnesium carbonate) which ultimately became the rock dolostone.

Only remnants of these Paleozoic strata are seen in the mountains around Banff and Jasper. In the Edmonton region and in eastern Alberta they were completely stripped away by erosion during Devonian time.

We know little about the period 438 to 380 million years ago in central Alberta, because few traces of Silurian or Lower Devonian rocks are available for study. This may be due to the fact that Alberta was at that time high and dry, the land having been lifted up above sea level. It was on this land, in early Devonian time, that the first land plants emerged. These plants were primitive clubmosses and lichens amongst which the first primitive insects flitted and crawled.

Upper Paleozoic strata are well represented in outcrop in Alberta. Below Edmonton and throughout much of Alberta marine strata of Middle and Late Devonian age (380 to 360 million years old) overlie the Precambrian basement floor. Once more the sea had broken over a natural barrier in northern Alberta and flooded southward into the region.

Again, the fact that limestones and dolostones constitute much of the Devonian succession indicates that this part of the North American continental plate still had not drifted northward out of the tropical climatic zone. The tropical waters nourished a profusion of life in the shallower parts of the sea. Among the many relatively new life forms were reef-building corals. These organisms need warm, clean, well-lit and aerated sea water and thrive only at depths shallower than 20 m. This arises because they depend upon a symbiotic relationship (close and mutually beneficial coexistence) with photosynthesizing microscopic blue-green algae. Corals therefore inhabit shallow coastal waters building underwater hills.

The incredible profusion of life in this Devonian sea led to the rapid accumulation of abundant animal and plant debris in the sediments of deeper waters. As time went by the rapidly buried organic material was attacked by bacteria in the sediments and subjected to temperatures of 75° to 125°C by burial metamorphism. The organic debris was gradually broken down and transformed into hydrocarbons capable of generating vast reserves of oil and natural gas. The same bacteria in the sediments also consumed sulphur-bearing organics and broke them down to produce hydrogen sulphide (H_2S) gas. This gas is a significant component in sour gas of Alberta and constitutes a very important raw material for the production of sulphur (Chapter 3).

Some of the reservoir rocks in which much of Alberta's oil and gas occur today are in part porous rocks of the ancient coral reefs. It is such porous and permeable reefal carbonate reservoirs that host the incredibly rich oil and gas accumulations at Rainbow Lake, Zama, Leduc-Woodbend, Redwater, Malmo, New Norway, etc.

Tropical Devonian seawaters were evaporated in shallow, isolated lagoons and thus large amounts of salt (sodium chloride), potash (potassium chloride) and gypsum (calcium sulphate) are found associated with the Devonian carbonate strata, both in Alberta and in Saskatchewan. These commodities too have played major roles in the economic development of Western Canadian resource industries.

During the Carboniferous Period, the sea-floor in parts of Alberta was tectonically uplifted, and for a short time the site of Alberta was eroded. But it was not long before subsidence once again brought the sea rushing in. This time, the sea was perhaps a little cooler and the water a little deeper. The prevailing conditions might have been somewhat like the present-day Bahamas Banks of the Caribbean. Carbonate debris (broken shells, corals and crinoid fragments) accumulated in shallower waters, washed in by tidal currents. In this way, porous and permeable limestones formed from these carbonate fragments also played important roles as oil and gas reservoirs e.g. at Turner Valley, Pincher Creek and Waterton. These shallow marine conditions predominated between 360 and 245 million years ago, at which time the region underwent a major phase of uplift and erosion, associated with plate movement which was dragging the west of Canada northward into cooler climates beyond 30° North.

◼ Mesozoic Era
– the docking of the continental ship

(245 to 67 million years ago)

During Triassic and Jurassic time, Alberta formed part of the western shoreline of the drifting and rising North American continent. The sea had withdrawn from the landmass to lie in the western part of the Province. Rivers fed the coastal waters with abundant sand and clay. Thus the temperate marine waters were no longer clear, but became turbid with sediment. By the end of Jurassic time, deltas and mud banks developed along the coasts. These marginal coastal sectors were poorly drained with profuse vegetation flourishing in swamps, and forested by cypress trees, cycads and conifers. Over thousands of years these trees flourished, died and fell rotting into the murky waters. This abundant decaying plant debris would later form some of Alberta's first coals. Travelling through the Crowsnest Pass into southern British Columbia one can see large mining operations extracting these Jurassic coals around Coalmont and Fernie.

About 140 million years ago, in the later part of the Jurassic Period, an offshore range of volcanic mountains, part of the primitive Cordillera, rose to form a barrier off the western coast. Thus, sediments flowed into the Alberta area both from the rising Cordillera to the west and from the eroding Shield to the east. The Cretaceous sea was at first an embayment extending from the north and later it became a complete inland seaway between the present Gulf of Mexico and the modern Arctic Ocean.

This was the beginning of the second era of great mountain building. The Rocky Mountains were being born due to the violent collision between the crust of the Pacific Ocean floor and the crust of the North American continent. The offshore mountains spewed lavas down their slopes. Great clouds of volcanic ash were thrown skyward and were blown inland over the Edmonton region. Thus, many of the inland deltas and swamps were often choked with ash, which can be seen today interbedded with many of the Cretaceous strata of the Edmonton region. They do not look like volcanic ash now, for time and weathering have changed them into sticky clay-rich rocks known as bentonites. The bentonitic clays are both a nuisance and a benefit. On the one hand, they cause many of our unpaved country roads to get very slippery in wet weather, and many of our riverside walks to be hazardous to the unwary walker who sinks into them, emerging with clay-laden footwear. Bentonites swell when wet and contribute to making many of the river banks unstable. Hence, it is common around Edmonton for landslips to occur after an early summer rainstorm. Walk from Emily Murphy Park sometime and take the riverside trail toward the High Level Bridge (Chapter 5). There you will see dozens of poplar trees leaning over at crazy angles, due to the slipping of bentonitic clay layers in the Cretaceous bedrock. On the other hand, bentonites have desirable properties which are of great benefit to society in that they are used as thickeners in drilling muds to aid in oil exploration and as impermeable clay linings for containing water in canals and waste within landfills (Chapter 4).

During Cretaceous time the environment of the Edmonton region rapidly changed as the region moved northwestward (Figure 3), grinding and bumping against the Pacific plate which was bulldozing it from the south. The region passed from a warmer climatic zone into latitudes of a cooler Mediterranean climate. In the sea, ammonites and clams thrived and marine dinosaurs and fish swam in abundance. On the land, thick vegetation flourished, with verdant forests nourished by abundant rainfall and the fertilizing volcanic ash which rained down regularly from the leaden skies. The forests, with magnolias, sycamores, figs, ferns, cycads, conifers, chestnuts and *Metasequoia sp.* (relatives of the California redwoods) covered the slopes and the swampy coastal plains. Here, as in Jurassic time, abundant rotting vegetation was accumulating and being rapidly buried in Everglade-type swamps. This rotting organic material has rewarded us with a spectrum of useful fossil-fuel commodities in the Edmonton region. Some of the organic material was transformed into peat and ultimately became coal and thus many parts of Alberta, including the City of Edmonton, were endowed with a supply of solid fossil fuels during the early periods of settlement (Chapter 3). Some of the deeper coal seams are now

being considered as future sources of methane (natural gas) production. Other masses of rotting organic debris were transformed into oil and gas, which are now present in many of the Cretaceous rocks of Alberta around Edmonton, Calgary, Drumheller and Fort McMurray. In these cases, the oil and gas have migrated not into carbonate rocks (limestones and dolostones), but into porous and permeable sandstone reservoir rocks.

In the forests and swamps of Cretaceous Alberta, the terrestrial and amphibious dinosaurs rose as rulers of the continent and its shallow marginal waters. It was here too that primitive primates, tiny shrew-like animals, crept meekly through the trees and bushes awaiting their time for development and evolutionary triumph. We can find traces of both the forests and of the dinosaurs all around Edmonton, wherever streams have cut down to expose the Cretaceous strata, e.g. in the North Saskatchewan River valley (Figure 4). Occasionally coal beds with plant fragments are found and we may be lucky enough to come across a bone or a tooth. To get a better idea of what the Edmonton region was like during the Cretaceous Period, visit the Royal Tyrrell Museum at Drumheller. There you can see the Cretaceous faunas depicted better than anywhere else in the world. You can also see the fossil floras displayed in a greenhouse and walk among tree species which have survived since Cretaceous time.

■ The End of an Era

The end of the Cretaceous Period, 67 million years ago, was marked by profound changes in Alberta. The mighty push of the Pacific plate folded and thrusted the rocks of British Columbia (which was at last a recognizable component of western North America). Volcanoes were still erupting in the western sectors of the Cordillera. The ramparts of the Rockies loomed for the first time on the western horizon of Alberta. Here, vast sheets of older rock were thrust upward and rammed into the edge of the sediment-filled Western Canada Basin, to form the fold belt of the Alberta Rockies and Foothills.

All this time the continent was moving slowly northward into cooler latitudes. Little wonder then that many animals and plants became extinct during this period of great change. With a cooling climate and a changing topography (which would commonly prevent rain-bearing clouds from penetrating the high mountains into Alberta), the overall environment experienced some major changes. Under cool, dry conditions the lush flora of the Cretaceous was killed off and in its place came grasses and sedges more suited to a cooler continental interior environment. These changes brought severe ecological pressures upon the life forms inhabiting Western Canada. Traditional food supplies dwindled and animals shivered under cold night skies. Those who did not adapt either migrated or died.

Various hypotheses deal with the extinction of the dinosaurs. These hypotheses have lately suggested that

Joseph Burr Tyrrell (1858-1957)

Joseph Tyrrell was a geologist, explorer and historian who surveyed vast areas of western and northern Canada. Tyrrell was born in Weston, Ontario (now part of Toronto) and graduated in Arts from the University of Toronto. After a short career in law, he joined the Geological Survey of Canada.

As a field assistant under G.M. Dawson, Tyrrell discovered the coal deposits of Fernie, B.C. From 1884 to 1887 he led his own expeditions to survey the area between the Bow and North Saskatchewan rivers. He made two major discoveries: coal deposits that would become the Drumheller coalfield and one of the world's greatest dinosaur collecting localities. The Royal Tyrrell Museum of Paleontology, built at Drumheller by the Alberta Government, is named after him. In 1887, Tyrrell described the rocks exposed along the North Saskatchewan River in the vicinity of Fort Edmonton and named them the Edmonton Formation.

In 1893-94 Tyrrell gained international fame for his explorations through the "Barren Lands" of the Northwest Territories. Leaving the Geological Survey in 1899, Tyrrell became a mining consultant in the Klondike before making his fortune in the Kirkland Lake gold camp of Ontario.

In 1915 Tyrrell published "Gold on the North Saskatchewan River" in the Transactions of the Canadian Mining Institute, in which he reviewed the history of mining in the Edmonton area and his views on the origin of the gold.

Tyrrell's interest in early Canadian explorers led him to edit the diaries of Samuel Hearne and David Thompson for publication by the Champlain Society.

Photo credit: Geological Survey of Canada

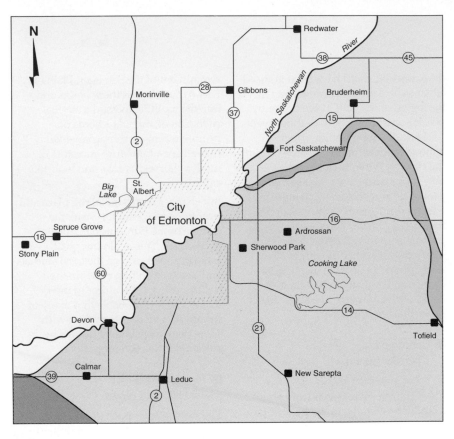

Tertiary and Cretaceous

 Paskapoo Formation
sandstone, siltstone; coal, tuff beds

Cretaceous

Wapiti Formation
sandstone, mudstone, shale; ironstone, coal

Horseshoe Canyon Formation
sandstone, mudstone, shale; ironstone, coal

Bearpaw Formation
silty shale, minor clayey sandstone

Belly River Formation
sandstone, siltstone, mudstone; ironstone

Figure 4. Bedrock geology of the Edmonton region.

the extinction could have been induced either by a giant meteorite impact in the region of the Gulf of Mexico or by volcanic eruptions. Both of these events could lead to long lasting upper atmospheric pollution and a cooling of the climate. While such hypotheses may prove correct, we can see that the geological and ecological changes in Alberta during the Cretaceous Period had already placed some severe pressures upon indigenous species of dinosaurs and other life forms. They really could not tolerate much more change and any other climatic shift could well have been "the straw that broke the dinosaur's back"!

■ Cenozoic Era
– familiar scenes

(67 million years to present)

The Cenozoic Era extends from about 67 million years ago to the present-day, and for this enormous span of time Alberta has been gradually developing the topographic character which it possesses today.

In the early Cenozoic, during the Tertiary Period, the Rocky Mountains were still being thrust into the western sectors of Alberta. As the mountains rose, they crumbled and were eroded. Vast sheets of detritus lay piled in front of the new mountains and spread over the plains of Alberta to their eastern reaches. These piles of detritus (termed molasse) are now seen as sands and gravels in the regions of Edson, Drayton Valley and Red Deer.

The plains of the Edmonton region were grasslands, enjoying a climate similar to that of Arizona today and

reminiscent of the Serengeti Plain of East Africa. Across these plains and into the foothills roamed a strange collection of animals – herds of primitive camels, rhinoceros-like titanotheres, miniature ancestors of modern horses, hyenas and wolf-like carnivores.

But changes were still taking place and over the next 65 million years the climate of the Edmonton region got even cooler. This again put great ecological pressure on the local animals and plants, resulting either in their withdrawal southward or in their extinction. It is probable that many of the animals were able to cope with some degree of climatic change by annual north-south migration.

■ Pleistocene Epoch
– a chill wind blows

The Pleistocene Epoch opened the Quaternary Period some 1.6 million years ago. Once more the region of Edmonton was about to experience some profound changes in climate. About 1 million years ago, the Arctic ice cap began to grow and its margin moved southward across the northern continents. At the same time, mountain glaciers grew and flowed down toward the Pacific coast and onto the plains of Western Canada.

There were actually four major glacial advances of Arctic ice into northern Canada. Between each major continental ice advance the ice recessed during a warmer, interglacial phase. But despite the advances, it was not until around 21,000 years ago during the last (Wisconsin) glacial advance that

Alberta became covered by ice. Until that time Alberta was ice-free and supported a boreal flora on its plains and hills. Across the grasslands and in the thin boreal scrub bush wandered bison, muskoxen, horses, woolly mammoths and mastodons.

During the Wisconsin glaciation most of Alberta (with the exception of the cap of the Cypress Hills) was draped by slow moving ice sheets. In the Edmonton area, far from the centre of the ice sheet, the plains were covered by up to 1.5 km of ice, which flowed from the north and northeast. This continental ice sheet met with Cordilleran valley glaciers flowing eastward out of the mountains, through the foothills and onto the plains. If one had been able to fly over the region at that time, the view would have been similar to interior Greenland or Antarctica today, with a vast ice field broken only by the occasional nunatak poking through the ice in southeastern and southwestern Alberta.

As these great sheets of ice flowed out and across the plains, they carried masses of rock and debris torn from the mountains or from the rocks of northern Alberta and beyond. Indeed, with their bases loaded with boulders and fragments of rock, these ice masses were the most powerful erosional agents to ever affect the region.

The melting of the Wisconsin glaciers began around 12,000 years ago and continues today in some of the slowly receding glaciers of the Rockies. As the glaciers melted they left behind a drastically modified landscape, bearing the erosive scars of glaciation and littered with the debris of destruction.

Where the heavy ice sheet had pressed down on the soft bedrock, many of the surficial strata were deformed and folded. Great slices of bedrock were bulldozed out and dumped by the ice (e.g. around Cooking Lake, east of Edmonton). The Prairies were covered by recessional moraines and tills. Pitted ground bears witness to the slow melting of enormous isolated blocks of ice buried within the glacial debris.

Cold adiabatic winds roared off the receding ice sheet and winnowed out finer particles to form loess and sand dune fields (e.g. near Devon and Fort Saskatchewan, Figure 12). As the ice melted, rivers of cold meltwater fed ice-dammed lakes which supported a sparse algal flora. Such lake sediment is the origin of the black, organic-rich soils which exist around Alberta. Occasionally the ice-dams would break and cold meltwater would rush out, carving a deep channel across the plains in a matter of days. Such glacial outlet channels are common throughout Alberta (e.g. the Gwynne Outlet channel east of Leduc (Figures 10, 12 and 13).

■ Recent Time

The recent (postglacial) geological history of Alberta is mainly a story of slow erosion by rivers which are modifying a newly deglaciated landscape. We commonly see clear evidence of uplift in the region in the form of alluvial terraces. This uplift is partly due to the fact that, while the 1.5 km thick Pleistocene ice sheet was covering the region, the land was pressed down under a tremendous load. Thus, when the ice sheet melted, the land rebounded isostatically (glacio-isostasy) in a series of relaxative jerks. Each time there was increased downcutting by the rivers and creeks as the flood plains were dissected. As the rivers eroded and resorted the materials of previous geological eras certain dense minerals became concentrated in the alluvium. Thus, gold and platinum, probably eroded from Cretaceous, Cenozoic and Pleistocene strata, are commonly concentrated in Alberta's river valleys (Chapter 3). The North Saskatchewan and McLeod Rivers were significant producers of placer gold and major contributors to local economies in the late 1800s and the mid-1900s.

Melting of the ice sheet left a landscape dotted with lakes, many of which have since dried up. Travelling through eastern Alberta, we commonly see dried up lake beds with extensive deposits of evaporitic salts. Many of these lakes were probably of pluvial type, and had originated during times of intense rainfall just after the Pleistocene ice withdrew. Such salt deposits (typically sodium sulphate) can be utilized for industrial purposes.

Since the Pleistocene ice melted away, the face of Alberta's desolate landscape became clothed in sub-boreal vegetation of various styles. The vegetation styles reflect the soils, bedrock, groundwater and surficial deposits underlying each area. For 10,000 years, nature has attained an ecological balance in each geographic sub-region of Alberta. But, for the past 150 years the presence of humankind has had some profound, and commonly negative effects on nature's designs. We can therefore count ourselves as the latest significant modifiers of Alberta's landscape.

Ice-Age Fossils

James A. Burns

For several decades there have been sporadic discoveries of bones and teeth of Quaternary Age (i.e. Ice Age) animals in the older gravels truncated by the North Saskatchewan River. Long considered to be of Tertiary Age and usually called "preglacial gravels" (Empress Formation), these deposits and their associated fossils are found in the buried-valley drainage system (Figure 16). Radiocarbon dates from bone proteins and from wood collected in local quarries indicate that these gravels were reworked during the late Quaternary Period. The term "preglacial" refers to gravels in the Edmonton area that do not contain rocks derived from the Canadian Shield, and therefore are thought not to have been brought by glaciers from the northeast. The inference is that these older gravels were transported eastward by rivers from the Rocky Mountains. The demonstrated presence of late Pleistocene animal and wood remains now requires wider acceptance

Provincial Museum of Alberta

Figure 5. Woolly mammoth.

Provincial Museum of Alberta

Figure 6. Sabre-toothed cat.

of a younger age for the reworked Empress Formation gravels; this part of the geological history of the Edmonton region can then be generally revised and updated.

Radiocarbon dates, including many supplied by the Isotope Laboratory of Alberta Environment in Vegreville, range from the practical upper limit of the method (about 40,000 years) to about 21,000 years ago. The existence of abundant grazing animals of this age suggests a comparable period of ice-free conditions in the Edmonton area conducive to a cool, dry grassland environment. These steppe-like conditions were associated with black spruce, larch, and sphagnum in the valleys.

Sometime after 21,000 years ago, the continental ice sheet advanced and submerged the region under 1 to 2 km of ice. Such ice was extensive, reaching west to the foothills and south beyond the Alberta/Montana border.

Around 12,000 years ago, the climate warmed and this ice sheet retreated past the Edmonton region. Meltwater and runoff dammed by the ice receding downslope (northeastward) caused ice-marginal lakes to form, like Glacial Lake Edmonton, the precise age of which remains unknown. It may have been very short-lived, perhaps less than 100 years. These lake sediments can be identified as the bedded, yellowish-beige, silty clay deposits at, or near, the top of the banks of the North Saskatchewan River. It was apparently not until about 11,600 years ago that animals returned to this region. In the wake of ice retreat, the abundant meltwater and channelled runoff initiated development of the present river valley. In the process, some of the preglacial gravels were rearranged and redeposited to include a scatter of animal and plant remains from both the preglacial and the subsequent postglacial recolonization.

Although not an exhaustive inventory of animal species, the list includes: horse, bison, muskox, camel, caribou, woolly mammoth (Figure 5), mastodon, ground sloth, lion, giant short-faced bear, sabre-toothed cat (Figure 6) and wolf. Tree remains include larch and spruce (probably the black spruce species).

Meteorites

Robert E. Folinsbee

The **Iron Creek** meteorite is the most famous of Alberta's meteorites. It is a 165 kg iron meteorite, with what appears to be a North American Indian's face when viewed in profile. It was recovered on a hill by the Blackfoot peoples and moved to a site where Iron Creek empties into the Battle River. Regarded by the missionaries as a graven image, but by the Indians as an immensely powerful Manitou stone, it was shipped to the mission in 1869, and eventually out of harm's way to Victoria College in Toronto. Great disaster later fell upon the Blackfoot tribes. The Iron Creek meteorite was eventually retrieved, and is now featured in the meteorite display at the Provincial Museum in Edmonton. Legend says this meteorite grew, and there is good evidence that the natives replaced the purloined iron with another meteorite from the same fall, even larger and too heavy to lift. Bill Mcdonald, as a boy, later an early geology graduate from the University of Alberta, saw an iron meteorite at Iron Creek at the turn of the century. It was surrounded with native bead offerings, and clearly was venerated. This iron too disappeared, perhaps buried to keep it from its brother's fate.

The City of Edmonton has its own meteorite, the **Edmonton** iron meteorite, which found its way into the University of Alberta geology collection. It was studied by John Allan, and is a rather rare type of iron meteorite, a hexahedrite. The University of Alberta collection grew with the acquisition of nearly all the fragments of the **Bruderheim** meteorite, a stony meteorite or chondrite. This fell on snowy frozen fields in 1960 and was picked up by local farmers and by Stan Walker and Ty Balacko of Fort Saskatchewan. The Bruderheim fall coincided with the beginning of the Apollo space program in U.S.A. and many researchers studied its fragments.

The gods struck again on March 31, 1963, with the fall of the **Peace River** meteorite, again on snowy fields. The late Lu Bayrock collected and interpreted sighting data, and following one of his recorded lines of sight John Westgate of the University of Alberta came up with Peace River Number 1, an 8 kg fragment supplemented by six other stones during the spring planting season when fields were being cultivated (Figure 7).

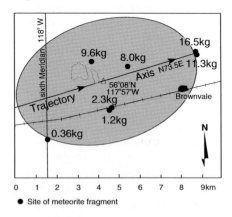

Figure 7. Peace River meteorite recoveries show concentrations of larger pieces in the direction of travel toward the far terminus of the ellipse of fall (data for September, 1963).

The **Vilna** meteorite, a bright bolide, was recorded on the Meanook all-sky camera of the Dominion Observatory on the evening of February 5, 1967. Only two small chips were recovered because the main fragments fell into a densely wooded area. The detonation was large and was recorded on the University of Alberta seismographs.

The **Mayerthorpe** meteorite is another find, also an iron meteorite, with four known fragments. One fragment was tossed back onto the field, another was used to hold a pigsty door closed. This latter fragment was subsequently housed in the University of Alberta meteorite collection.

The MORP project (Meteorite Observation and Recovery Program) grew out of the apparent frequency of falls and recoveries in Western Canada and eventually netted the **Innisfree** meteorite to Ian Halliday of the Dominion Observatory. The Innisfree meteorite has a well-documented orbit, one of only three orbits with the associated recovered meteorite known in the world. The Innisfree stones came from fragments perturbed out of the asteroid belt into an Earth-crossing orbit. The event may be a small cousin of the asteroid impact that is said to have caused the demise of the dinosaurs at the close of the Cretaceous Period.

Geomorphology   John Shaw

▄ Prairie Landscape
– setting the scene

Geomorphology (*geo* - Earth, *morphos* - shape, form) is the study of landforms which are the foundation of landscape; soils and plants, farmyards and fields, and roads and cities decorate the geomorphological landscape. We must go back in time to understand the present landscape: the hills are not everlasting, and "Old Man River" may not be so old; in short, the landscape is constantly changing. This change is largely imperceptible when measured against a human life span, but it can race along in the context of geological time.

The story begins in the Tertiary Period when the Rocky Mountains were just emerging. When the "Battle of the Rockies" was at its fiercest, snow and ice, wind and rain contrived to wear down the rising mountains, and mountain torrents carved deep valleys. The battle debris, gravel, sand and silt, was spread to the east in a vast alluvial apron criss-crossed by multi-channelled rivers.

For our first glimpse of the modern landscape of the Edmonton region, we see a vast river plain or fan sloping very gently upward to the west, its apex pointing to a deep valley cut through the foothills and mountain ranges. However, the battle was carried by the forces of erosion; rivers, which had first aggraded their beds, later on carried away more gravel and sand than they delivered. Deposition gave way to erosion; rivers cut down into the gravel plain. Thus, a dramatic change in the direction of landscape evolution began several million years ago in response to continued pulses of Rocky Mountain uplift.

We can only imagine the earlier depositional landscape, because so little of it has survived millions of years of erosion. Well-rounded quartzite pebbles in gravels capping the Cypress Hills, Swan Hills and Hand Hills, are some of the last surviving remnants of those earlier fluvial deposits. Our imaginative reconstruction of the landscape is based on the fact that the quartzitic pebbles and boulders must have originated in the mountains where quartzitic bedrock is common, and on the sedimentary characteristics of the gravel, which record deposition by fast-flowing, braided rivers that flowed from the west.

In time, uplift of the Rocky Mountains slowed, the sediment supply decreased, and the sediment-starved rivers cut even deeper, through the fan sediments of the Western Plains and into the underlying bedrock. New slopes were cut and fresh rock was exposed to the elements and broken down by cycles of wetting and drying and of freezing and thawing (known as mechanical weathering), and by acidic rainwater, groundwater and organic complexes (known as chemical weathering). Hundreds of metres of river gravel and rock were stripped from the Western Plains by these processes and carried to the Atlantic Ocean and to the great deltas of the

Mississippi and Mackenzie Rivers. So it was that the Western Plains and the broad, preglacial valleys came about by millions of years of weathering, slope erosion, and fluvial sediment transport. Only isolated upland plateaus, protected by resistant gravel caps, stand today as tiny remnants of an earlier vast depositional plains landscape.

The almost flat-lying bedrock strata beneath the Western Plains influence the shaping of this land, creating the distinctive landscape with its wide vistas over seemingly endless plains, broken only by deep valleys or where escarpments mark the surface expression of underlying more resistant beds. By contrast, where the bedrock which underlies the plains is folded and thrust, alternating beds of sandstone and shale, resistant and weak rocks, respectively, are exposed at the ground surface. Differential erosion of these rocks has sculpted the cuestas and vales that make the Foothills terrain so distinctive.

■ Glaciers Approach – falling temperatures and gravel deposition

In the Edmonton region, the bedrock erosional landscape described above is buried beneath glacial deposits which thicken where they infill preglacial river valleys (Figure 16). Preglacial rivers flowing in these valleys deposited sand and gravel of the Empress Formation which must underlie the younger glacial deposits (Figures 8 and 14). These earlier rivers were probably braided streams in broad valleys, unlike the present-day

Photograph by John D. Godfrey

Figure 8. Preglacial sands and gravels, Empress Formation (A) below glacial till (B), Clover Bar, Edmonton. The extremely sharp contact between the two deposits indicates glacial erosion removed sand and gravel before till was deposited.

North Saskatchewan River with its single channel deeply incised into a narrow valley.

Why did the preglacial rivers flowing through the Edmonton region change from an erosional to a depositional regime and aggrade their beds? The answer probably lies in climatic change, another factor in landscape evolution. Ice wedges, which grew as the gravels accumulated, appear in the Empress Formation as wedge forms infilled with younger sediment. They can be seen in any of the local gravel pits where the gravels are quarried, and they testify to the cold winters and permafrost at the time the Empress Formation was deposited in the Edmonton area.

Today, ice wedges are found only where permafrozen ground repeatedly contracts and fractures because of intense cold. Water seeps into the fractures where it freezes to form wedges below the permafrost table.

The date of approximately 40,000 to 22,000 years BP (Before Present), obtained from bone and wood radiometric dates, places the time of Empress Formation gravel deposition in the late Wisconsin glacial period, when the global climate was cold.

At that time, the accumulations of snow and ice in the mountains fed majestic valley glaciers. Now, only small valley glaciers and ice caps survive in today's relatively warm climate. We can surmise that erosion by alpine glaciers increased the amount of sediment supplied to the preglacial North Saskatchewan River, causing deposition of the Empress Formation in its valley at Edmonton. Clearly, a change in one aspect of the environment triggers a chain reaction in others. A climatic change caused glaciation; alpine glaciers increased the sediment supply to rivers; and the rivers responded by depositional infilling of their valleys. Although environmental change is now a fashionable topic, it is certainly not a new one. Nor is it always detrimental; the cost of building in Edmonton is considerably reduced because sand and gravel suitable for construction was delivered to the city's doorstep free of charge – by rivers flowing from the mountains to the west and by the Laurentide Ice Sheet flowing from the northeast.

■ Beneath the Ice Sheet

Glacial till, a heterogeneous mixture of fine and coarse sediment with virtually no visible stratification, records the advance of a massive continental ice sheet through the Edmonton region (Figure 8). At first glance, till appears to be an uninteresting, homogeneous glacial sediment. On closer

examination, however, a great deal can be learned about how the till was transported, deposited and where it came from. A number of clues from the till around Edmonton point to transport of glacial debris by the Laurentide Ice Sheet originating over Hudson Bay (Figure 9). This conclusion is based on several facts:

- Numerous till boulders (erratics) are from the Canadian Shield far to the northeast. Because rivers cannot flow up hill, these boulders must have been carried by another form of transport – *a continental ice sheet.*

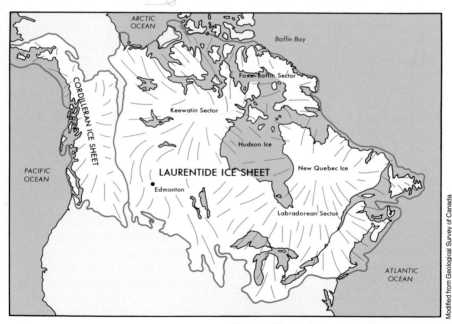

Figure 9. The maximum extent of ice over North America during the last continental glaciation (late Wisconsin).

- Many boulders are too large to have been transported by rivers across the plains, but there is no such size limitation on boulders transported by ice sheets.
- Some smooth, polished faces on boulders are worn flat and deeply scratched or striated, like boulders carried by glaciers in the Rockies today.
- Grooves, aligned north northeast to south southwest, were gouged into underlying sand, presumably by boulders protruding at the base of the moving ice sheet.
- Elongate rocks in the till are commonly aligned north northeast to south southwest, recording the southwestward flow of the ice sheet.

The till rests directly on surfaces cut into either Cretaceous bedrock or the Empress Formation sands and gravels. Stream deposits that now outline former meltwater channels below and within the till represent a former labyrinth of meltwater tunnels within and at the base of the ice sheet. Unfortunately for municipal engineers, who must anticipate bad ground conditions such as unusual groundwater pressures and unstable "soft till", these water-saturated sandy fluvial channels within the till are entirely unpredictable.

It has long been known that the Pleistocene Epoch or "Ice Age" involved several cycles of glacial advance and retreat: the most extensive events took place in the last 900,000 years. Consequently, it is surprising to discover that the great North American continental ice sheets reached the Edmonton region for the first time only recently. The evidence for this conclusion is difficult to ignore: if there had been earlier ice sheets from the Canadian Shield entering the Edmonton area, they would have carried Shield type rocks with them, and these would have been subsequently reworked by rivers. But the youngest deposits of the Empress Formation, deposited about 22,000 years ago, contain no pebbles of Shield rocks. Therefore, continental ice sheets did not reach the Edmonton area prior to about 22,000 years ago. There is no simple explanation for this remarkable conclusion which, at the very least, reminds us that little in terms of geological history can be taken for granted.

Most of the landforms associated with the Laurentide Ice Sheet around Edmonton are meltwater stream and glacial lake features, rather than glacial forms (Figure 10). The Cooking Lake Moraine, seen by thousands of visitors each year at Elk Island Park, is a spectacular exception. This moraine formed on high ground, where the ice sheet stagnated and melted away, leaving a steeply rolling topography of ridges and knolls arranged in a random pattern. Hundreds of lakes, ponds and sloughs are attractive features of the area. They occupy depressions left where the last isolated blocks of ice, enclosed within the glacial till, melted.

In contrast to the stagnant ice landforms of the Cooking Lake Moraine, the hills around Lake Wabamun and the Pigeon Hills north of Pigeon Lake reveal the full force of an active ice sheet. These hills resulted

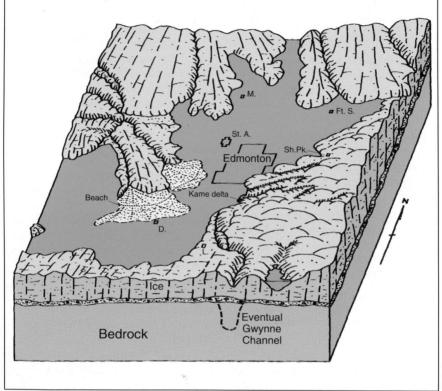

Bedrock

Ice

Eventual Gwynne Channel

Beach

Kame delta

Edmonton

St. A.

Sh.Pk.

M.

Ft. S.

D.

N

J.D. Godfrey

Figure 10. The Edmonton region during the final stages of deglaciation. The landscape is dominated by Glacial Lake Edmonton and stagnant dead ice. The location of the future Gwynne Outlet is shown.

from bedrock freezing and attaching to the base of the Laurentide Ice Sheet. Immense shear stresses exerted by the flowing ice sheet ripped out great slabs of bedrock which were folded by compression and thrust upward by the forward motion of the ice. This process is termed glaciotectonics, and is the only reasonable explanation for the hills and the deformed stratified bedrock within them.

We are just beginning to appreciate the possible importance to the Alberta landscape of meltwater action beneath the Laurentide Ice Sheet. According to a new and controversial interpretation, satellite images and air photographs carry evidence of a huge meltwater sheet flood that flowed over the Western Plains and across the regional slope, carving gigantic channels and forming fields of giant flutings (Figure 11). Only running water beneath an ice sheet could have both produced these forms and flowed upslope. The flood duration must have been limited to a few weeks, before the huge flows exhausted the subglacial meltwater reservoir. Adherents of the flood hypothesis argue that, in those few weeks, several thousand cubic kilometres of rock and sediment were stripped from the Plains – more than in the succeeding 15,000 years!

Satellite Image courtesy Remote Sensing Centre

Figure 11. Sharply defined parallel ridges (giant flutings) south of the Athabasca River are left upstanding when the intervening troughs were scoured by enormous subglacial floods. Athabasca townsite is located at the bend of the river (bottom left).

■ Ice Retreat
– a time for action

As the ice sheet retreated towards the northeast, we should visualize a massive ice dam that blocked the natural northeastward drainage and impounded meltwater to form Glacial Lake Edmonton. Meltwater rivers from the ice sheet deposited huge volumes of sediment into this glacial lake. Coarse, water-laid deposits, mainly sand, were deposited near to the ice front in "kames" (Figure 12). The "pitted delta" at Winterburn (Figure 10) marks the deposition of sand and silt on, and perhaps beneath, a large mass of stagnant ice. The former glacial lake bed extends over most of the Edmonton region and consists of bedded fine-grained silt and clays deposited from suspension in still waters of the lake. This fine-grained *glaciolacustrine* sediment is the cause of cracked basements and forms the notorious mud (*gumbo*). It also prompts tales of cars becoming mired in the deep ruts and thick mud of the City streets and when residents, on their way to work downtown, hid their mud-caked rubber boots beneath the boardwalk where they boarded the street car.

Glacial Lake Edmonton was short lived, and its end was probably as dramatic an event as any in the geological history of the region. Release of these lake waters was catastrophic. They scoured the glacial deposits down to bedrock at the head of a deeply incised valley (Gwynne Outlet) to the south of the City (Figure 13). Airline passengers can get a spectacular view of the Gwynne Outlet where it contains the linear-shaped Saunders, Ord and Coal Lakes, just southeast of the Edmonton International Airport.

Let us reconstruct this drainage event. Outflow from the ice-dammed lake forced its way beneath thinning ice at a topographic low point on the divide between the North Saskatchewan River and the Battle River. The discharge increased rapidly as the outlet size was enlarged by meltwater erosion of both the channel bed and overlying ice. As the flow increased so did the rate of erosion. Huge blocks of ice broke away from the ice sheet and were carried off in the flood. Picture a valley 1 km wide and 50 m deep, filled to its rims by a raging flood of muddy water choked with icebergs as big as three-storey houses. At maximum flow the Gwynne Outlet channel carried about a thousand times the mean flow of the North Saskatchewan River. The glacial lake was probably drained in a few days which, by the geological clock, is merely an instant of time. Those who know this story view the short history of the Gwynne Outlet with wonder and awe, sensing the powerful forces of natural events.

Drainage of the glacial lake caused its sediments, mainly lake-bed muddy silts and beach sand, to dry out and to be exposed to storm winds. The finer sediment was carried far out of the area, probably to the oceans. Wind-blown sand did not travel as far, and was redeposited in nearby dune fields like the one just north of Devon. Buried soils exposed in the numerous sand pits of the Devon dune field form conspicuous, dark organic layers, representing the vegetated surfaces of inactive, stable dunes. The sand which buried these *palaeosols* indicates renewed sand transport and dune reactivation, perhaps under relatively dry climatic conditions.

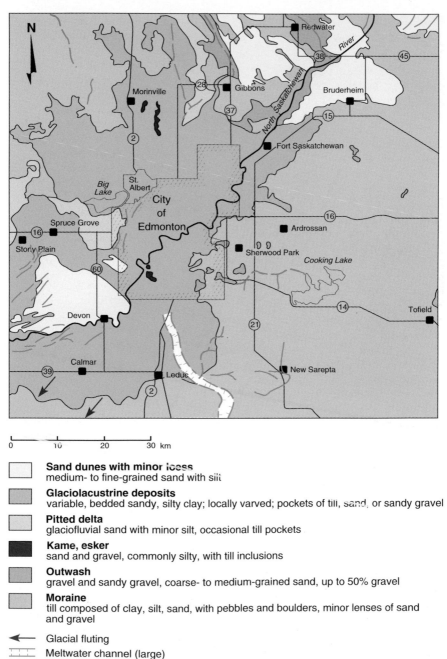

0   10   20   30 km

Sand dunes with minor loess
medium- to fine-grained sand with silt

Glaciolacustrine deposits
variable, bedded sandy, silty clay; locally varved; pockets of till, sand, or sandy gravel

Pitted delta
glaciofluvial sand with minor silt, occasional till pockets

Kame, esker
sand and gravel, commonly silty, with till inclusions

Outwash
gravel and sandy gravel, coarse- to medium-grained sand, up to 50% gravel

Moraine
till composed of clay, silt, sand, with pebbles and boulders, minor lenses of sand and gravel

← Glacial fluting

Meltwater channel (large)

Meltwater channel (small)

Figure 12. Surficial geology of the Edmonton region.

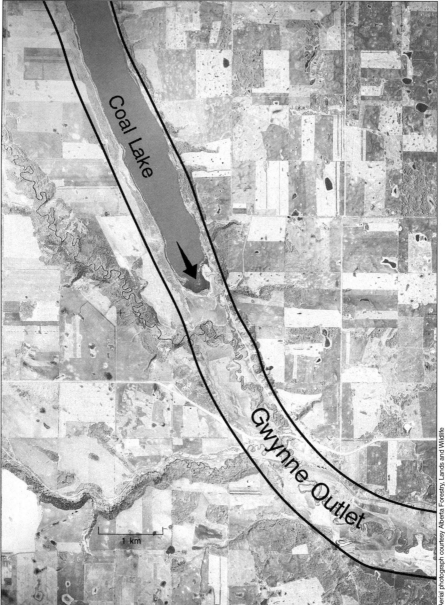

Figure 13. Aerial photograph of the Gwynne Outlet
near the hamlet of Gwynne. Meltwater from
Glacial Lake Edmonton eroded this channel,
probably in a few days! The sidewalls of the valley
are indicated.

Aerial photograph courtesy Alberta Forestry, Lands and Wildlife

■ Return of the River

The present valley of the North Saskatchewan River in the Edmonton region is very young; its excavation began less than 12,000 years ago, following the drainage of Glacial Lake Edmonton. At first, stream downcutting predominated over lateral erosion to produce a relatively deep, narrow river valley. In more recent times the river has widened its valley by undercutting and slumping of the steep walls. Erosion continues today, producing steep cliffs where flow impinges on the valley sides at the outside of bends. This erosion is balanced by deposition on the inside of bends, which builds broad flood plains and point bars. In places the river is a threat; some of the most serious problems of slope failure in the City are caused where the river undercuts the valley wall at the outside of bends (see viewpoint from Ada Boulevard, Site 8 of Chapter 5). In other places, such as Hawrelak Park and the districts of Rossdale and Riverdale, urbanization has taken advantage of the level ground of the flood plain, although the residential communities are at risk from flooding.

River terraces are remnants of former flood plains which were abandoned as the river cut down. There are four terrace levels in the Edmonton region (Figure 14): each one preserves river deposits. Bison bones found by Bruce Rains and Jim Welsh in the highest terrace deposits, about 55 m above the modern channel bed, give dates indicating that the valley floor was at that level about 11,000 years ago. Downcutting by the river was very rapid for about the next 3000 years. The modern flood plain, which is also the lowest terrace, began to form after this period of rapid incision. Sediments of the active flood plain contain bone and wood dating back about 8000 years, as well as mud deposited by the most recent overbank floods of this century. The evidence of little downcutting for most of postglacial time confirms our suspicion that, at present, the river is mainly working sideways and widening its valley.

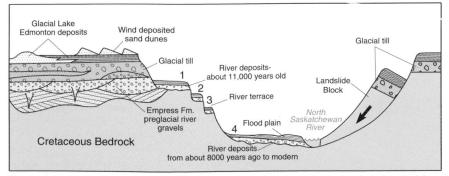

Figure 14. Idealized cross-section of North Saskatchewan River valley, showing four levels (ages) of river terraces, plus the preglacial and glacial deposits. This river valley did not exist 12,000 years ago.

In addition to the record of past floods, the fine-grained flood plain sediments also contain the record of one of the most spectacular volcanic eruptions in North America. About 6800 years ago, Mount Mazama in Oregon exploded, blowing the top of the mountain away and leaving a deep crater, now occupied by Crater Lake. Ash from this explosion was carried northeastward and blanketed much of southern Alberta. This ash is preserved, in a few places, as a layer less than 1 cm thick in the North Saskatchewan River flood plain deposits (Chapter 5).

Much of the glacial geology of the Edmonton region was first systematically mapped by L.A. Bayrock and his co-workers at the Alberta Research Council during the 1950s and 1960s.

Luboslaw (Lu) Antin Bayrock (1930-1989)

Photo: John D. Godfrey

Lu Bayrock was the first research Quaternary geologist at the Alberta Research Council and was responsible for producing the majority of the Council's primary surficial geology maps. Bayrock was born in the Ukraine and came to Edmonton shortly after World War II. He received his academic training at the University of Alberta and the University of Wisconsin.

Bayrock joined the Alberta Research Council in 1953 as a part of its new Glacial Geology program. His mapping skills were legendary; he produced maps covering 260,000 km^2 during his career at the Council. In 1962 Bayrock produced the first detailed report on the surficial geology of the Edmonton region. During the field research, he became aware of the wealth of Pleistocene fossils in the Edmonton region. He organized the gravel pit operators into collecting some of this fossil material, amassing a collection of 40 bison skulls.

Bayrock was interested in all aspects of geology and in a number of related fields. His numerous mapping projects brought him in contact with teepee rings, boulder effigies, and a variety of other native artifacts that led him to become a founding member of the Archaeological Society of Alberta. Bayrock had a strong interest in meteorites, and he took an active leading role in the recovery of the Peace River, Bruderheim and Vilna meteorites.

Bayrock left the Research Council in 1972 to start his own consulting firm. His experience in mapping glacial erratics allowed him to make a significant contribution to the discovery of the Key Lake and Maurice Bay uranium deposits of northern Saskatchewan.

Groundwater

Richard Stein

■ What is Groundwater?

Groundwater is arguably our most important Earth resource, but is commonly poorly understood. Except for lakes, streams, springs and water wells, it is for the most part hidden from view and thus shrouded in mystery. People still commonly speak of groundwater as occurring in underground lakes, streams or veins, which can be found only by "water witchers" or "diviners". In this section we try to dispel some of the mystery and show how and where usable groundwater can be found in the Edmonton region, using scientific information and methods.

Groundwater occupies the voids (pore spaces and fractures) in rocks that lie within the *saturated zone* beneath the *water table*. The water table commonly lies only a few metres below the ground surface in the plains regions of Alberta. Generally, the surface of the water table is not flat, but is a subdued replica of the overlying surface topography. The water table tends to be slightly deeper in upland areas and shallower in low-lying areas. This situation may be reversed in areas of local high relief, such as the hummocky moraines east of Edmonton (Figure 10). In the plains region, sloughs, creeks and lakes generally occur where the water table comes to the surface and this surface water may be thought of as "outcrops" of the water table.

Under the influence of gravity, groundwater is in constant motion beneath the ground surface. It flows underground from high to low elevations. The groundwater system is replenished, or *recharged*, by a portion of rain and melted snow which seeps into the ground in upland areas and is removed, or *discharged*, in lower-lying areas.

Groundwater moves extremely slowly, when compared to runoff or surface streams. The rate of movement is governed by two factors: the *permeability* of the geological materials containing the groundwater, and the *hydraulic gradient*. Highly permeable materials, such as gravel or coarse sand, permit groundwater to move much more easily than tighter till or lacustrine clay, which are typically composed of low-permeability materials. The hydraulic gradient results from differences in elevation of the water table surface at different places. Where these elevation differences are great, the groundwater moves rapidly. Where there is little relief on the water table surface, the groundwater movement is slow.

Permeability (otherwise referred to as *hydraulic conductivity*) is measured in units of velocity, for example metres per second. This represents the speed at which water travels through a given geological material under a specific hydraulic gradient. The hydraulic gradient is simply the change in elevation of the water level (or loss in hydraulic head) as groundwater moves over a given distance.

The various combinations of hydraulic conductivity and hydraulic gradient in the subsurface generate a wide variation in groundwater flow velocities. For example, in a clean sand, groundwater may flow at a velocity of about 0.4 m/day, or 100 m/year. On the other hand, in an unweathered till, the velocity may be only around 0.00004 m/day, or about 15 mm/year. Thus, groundwater would take 600 to 700 years to move through 10 m of such sediment! Therefore, compared with surface streams, groundwater moves very slowly indeed.

Because groundwater moves so very slowly, its age or the time elapsed since it entered the water table, can be very great. Water contained within deeply buried Pleistocene till or glaciolacustrine clay may be the same water that was incorporated with the sediment at the time of deposition, some 12,000 to 18,000 years ago. Consequently, water drawn from a well in the Edmonton region today could have originated as rain or snow that fell centuries, or even millennia ago!

■ Good Water, Bad Water

On its journey through the subsurface, groundwater encounters many kinds of rocks and minerals which are water-soluble to various degrees. Halite, common salt, is highly soluble to the extent of 250,000 mg/l (milligrams/litre); gypsum (calcium suphate) dissolves up to 2500 mg/l, and calcite (calcium carbonate) in the range of 100 to 200 mg/l. Silicate minerals are much less soluble, and it is uncommon to find more than 15 mg/l of silica dissolved in groundwater.

Nearly all mineral constituents dissolved in water are present in ionic form. Negatively charged ions are known as *anions;* positively charged ions, as *cations*. Our local groundwater is dominated by a few major cations and anions, namely: calcium (Ca^{2+}), magnesium (Mg^{2+}), sodium (Na^+), bicarbonate (HCO_3-), sulphate ($SO_4$2-) and chloride (Cl^-). Calcium and magnesium ions cause water to be "hard"; soaps and detergents do not lather readily and bath-tubs and showers get that annoying soap-scum film on them. In contrast, sodium ions cause water to be "soft".

How do the various ions get into the groundwater? We are all aware of acid rain caused by atmospheric pollution. But acidic rainwater has been produced under natural conditions since time immemorial. Falling rain dissolves carbon dioxide (CO_2) and other natural atmospheric gases, causing the water to become slightly acidic. The infiltration of this acidic rainwater into soil dissolves additional CO_2 generated in the root zone of plants, both from decay of organic matter and root respiration. Thus, the soil moisture becomes even more acidic. The acidic infiltration water effectively dissolves carbonate rocks (limestone, dolostone) and minerals (calcite and dolomite), breaking them down to release calcium, magnesium, and bicarbonate ions.

Other ions are dissolved as chemical reactions take place whilst groundwater flows through the rocks. For example, sulphate ions are added by contact with such minerals as gypsum ($CaSO_4 \bullet 2H_2O$), pyrite (FeS_2), or weathered sulphur-rich organic compounds. The sulphate ions may be reduced by sulphur-loving bacteria to give off the "bad-egg" gas hydrogen sulphide (H_2S). Groundwater reacts with clays, leading to adsorbtion of calcium and magnesium and the simultaneous release of sodium during a cation-exchange process. Chloride ions are commonly assimilated as groundwater passes through marine sedimentary rocks which still contain marine salts.

The chemical character of groundwater in the Edmonton region varies according to the nature of the subsurface geology. Very shallow groundwater in upland recharge areas of glacial drift has high calcium, magnesium and bicarbonate content. As water infiltrates down through thin drift or bedrock, dissolution of gypsum, oxidation of pyrite and weathering of organic-rich carbonaceous rocks result in the addition of sulphate, whereas calcium and magnesium are exchanged for sodium on the clay mineral lattices. Naturally occurring anaerobic sulphur-loving bacteria use oxygen from the sulphate to transform sulphate into bicarbonate plus hydrogen sulphide gas. Thereby, sulphate content is decreased and bicarbonate content is increased. Finally, chloride ions are dissolved by groundwater from the deeper salt-bearing sedimentary rocks.

Knowing the pattern of chemical change along the flow path of groundwater in the Edmonton region, it is possible to predict the quality of groundwater for an area where a water well might be drilled for domestic, agricultural or industrial purposes.

■ Where to Drill

To be of practical use as a source of water, groundwater must be available in sufficient amounts to meet the needs of the particular purpose or project. Geological formations that are porous and permeable enough to allow significant water withdrawals are known as *aquifers*. Where are such aquifers to be found beneath the Edmonton region?

Two types of aquifer occur. They differ with respect to both the amount and quality of available groundwater. These aquifers are found within:
1. Cretaceous bedrock, and
2. surficial deposits.

■ Groundwater in Cretaceous Bedrock

Bedrock aquifers that are important in meeting the various needs of the Edmonton region are found in sediments laid down in non-marine environments during Late Cretaceous time. These strata include the Wapiti, Belly River and Horseshoe Canyon Formations, all of which overlie a marine shale known as the Lea Park Formation (Figure 15). For practical purposes, this impermeable 250 m thick marine shale is the depth limit for useful groundwater exploration and development in the Edmonton region.

Cretaceous bedrock above the Lea Park Formation consists of non-marine shales, siltstones, sandstones and numerous coal beds termed the Wapiti Formation north of the North Saskatchewan River, and the Belly River and Horseshoe Canyon

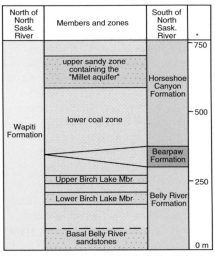

North of North Sask. River	Members and zones	South of North Sask. River	*
			750
Wapiti Formation	upper sandy zone containing the "Millet aquifer"	Horseshoe Canyon Formation	
	lower coal zone		500
		Bearpaw Formation	
	Upper Birch Lake Mbr		250
	Lower Birch Lake Mbr	Belly River Formation	
	Basal Belly River sandstones		0 m

* Height in metres above base of the Belly River Formation

Figure 15. Bedrock formations and their main aquifer zones above the Upper Cretaceous Lea Park Formation.

Formations in the region south of the North Saskatchewan River. Marine shales and sandstones between the Belly River and Horseshoe Canyon Formations are known as the Bearpaw Formation (Figure 15).

An important consideration regarding groundwater exploration in the Edmonton region is the structure of the Cretaceous bedrock strata. The average regional dip is to the southwest at 1 in 250 to 1 in 350. Therefore, any particular bed is more deeply buried downdip toward the southwest. Knowledge of the regional structure allows us to predict the depth and quality, or potability, of groundwater within individual aquifers. Groundwater is invariably less mineralized, and hence more potable, updip toward the subcrop (i.e. toward

the surface) of individual aquifers. Chemical quality and potability decrease dramatically as individual beds are more deeply buried. Thus, southwest of Edmonton, wells must be confined to the shallow portions of the Cretaceous strata.

Several sandstone and coal beds above the Lea Park Formation are important with respect to groundwater production, namely:

Zone 1: Two zones of sandstone beds in the upper part of the *Belly River Formation* (the Lower and Upper Birch Lake Members). The zones have numerous discontinuous sandstone beds of relatively high permeability ranging from 3 to 9 m in thickness.

Birch Lake Member sandstones are the most commonly used aquifers within a band extending northwest from Mundare to Bruderheim, to 3 to 10 km south of Redwater, and beyond (Figure 16). You can see these sandstone beds in outcrop along the north bank of the North Saskatchewan River, 2.5 to 3 km south of Amelia, near Bruderheim.

The production capability of the Birch Lake Members is about 0.4 l/s (litres/second) near Mundare; 0.6 l/s at Bruderheim; 1.1 l/s 5 km west of Bruderheim; and up to 25 l/s south of Redwater. Along the northwest trend from Redwater, water wells produce in the range of 0.4 to 4 l/s. The Lower Birch Lake Member sandstones have long been important aquifers for community, agricultural, and domestic users where they are shallow enough to be drilled economically. Areas where this aquifer yields more than 0.4 l/s are shown in Figure 16.

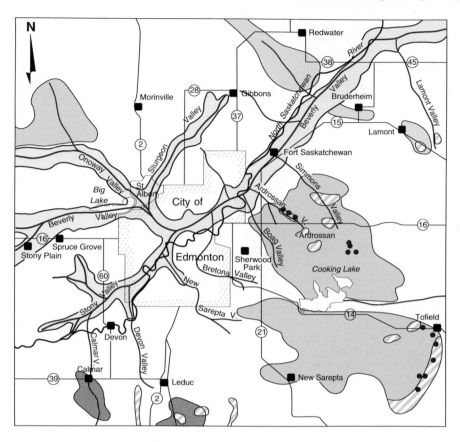

Thalweg of preglacial buried valley

Extent of buried valley aquifers (mainly Empress Formation)

Formations and rock types comprising main bedrock aquifers

Upper Horseshoe Canyon Formation (fractured sandstone)

Lower Horseshoe Canyon Formation (coal seams)

Birch Lake Member (sandstones)

Area of flowing wells

• Spring

Figure 16. The preglacial buried-valley system of the Edmonton region, the main bedrock aquifers and other groundwater features.

Groundwater in these aquifers is generally of excellent quality, with a *total dissolved solids* (TDS) content of less than 1000 mg/l at depths as great as 75 m. Chemically, the water is generally of the sodium-bicarbonate type and contains only minor amounts of the sulphate and chloride ions, which impart unfavorable chemical characteristics to groundwater in other parts of the Edmonton region.

Zones 2 and 3: *The Horseshoe Canyon Formation* was deposited in a largely swampy, deltaic environment which was occasionally flooded by the sea. The lowermost 150 m of this formation contain as many as 12 coal seams, and where these coals are fractured they constitute important aquifers. Bentonitic sandstones in the formation have low permeability (due to a high content of swelling-clay), and thus make poor or unpredictable aquifers. The interfingering of these lens-shaped strata in the ancient delta causes groundwater conditions to differ sharply over very short distances. The brackish water environment in which some of the strata were deposited results in high TDS and high chloride content in the groundwater from relatively deeply buried (greater than 75 m) parts of the formation.

Two parts of the Horseshoe Canyon Formation are important with respect to groundwater availability. These are the lower part, containing fractured coal seams (Zone 2), and the upper part, about 45 to 120 m below the top of the formation, which contains fractured, non-bentonitic sandstone beds (Zone 3). Wells completed in either of these sections of the formation are generally capable of producing

groundwater at rates ranging from 0.4 to 7.5 l/s. Wells completed in other parts of the Horseshoe Canyon Formation generally produce less than 0.4 l/s, and in some places cannot produce sufficient water for even domestic supplies. Areas in which the Horseshoe Canyon Formation is capable of yielding more than 0.4 l/s are shown on Figure 16.

The belt underlain by the subcrop zone of coal seams is shown in Figure 16. This belt extends northwest from the Cooking Lake Moraine Upland, across the valleys of the North Saskatchewan River and Sturgeon River. Within this belt, the most important and highly productive coal aquifers are found beneath the Cooking Lake Moraine. This is fortunate because a plentiful water supply is needed for the extensive residential acreages developed in the area. It is estimated that about 75 percent of the acreages use well water from these coal seams.

It has been suggested that coal seams beneath the Cooking Lake Moraine are more productive than equivalent seams elsewhere because they are more highly fractured, and that these fractures were caused by glacial overriding and bedrock deformation. The fractures may be better developed because the prominent elevation of the bedrock beneath the Cooking Lake Moraine provided a greater barrier and resistance to the advancing ice sheet. Therefore, it was more deformed than the surrounding lower areas. Fractures in the coal seams diminish dramatically with depth and are generally not apparent at depths greater than about 60 m, so that even thick coal seams are not significant water producers at depths greater than 60 m. Thus, the most productive wells in the area (up to 8 l/s) are generally less than about 45 m deep. Wells at greater depths, from 45 to 60 m, produce between 0.5 to 2 l/s.

Water from the coal aquifers is generally of acceptable quality, being of the sodium – bicarbonate type and having a TDS content between 1000 and 1500 mg/l. However, most of the water from these coal aquifers has a high iron content that requires treatment for iron removal.

The Zone 3 fractured sandstones from 45 to 125 m below the top of the Horseshoe Canyon Formation constitute the main bedrock aquifer for the communities of Millet, Calmar and Kavanagh and the farms that surround them (Figure 16). Water produced from these sandstones, is generally of excellent chemical quality with a TDS content of less than 1000 mg/l, major ions of sodium and bicarbonate, and contains only minor amounts of the objectionable sulphate ion.

■ Groundwater in Surficial Deposits

The topography of the bedrock surface underlying the surficial deposits in the Edmonton region is largely the result of long-term erosion through the late Tertiary and early Pleistocene. This buried, older erosional surface is very similar to the present-day topography. That is, the present-day major uplands and lowlands generally coincide with those of preglacial time. Just as today, the headwaters of the preglacial rivers were also in the mountains to the west and flowed toward the east and northeast. Coarse fluvial sediments

(gravel and sand, along with minor silt and clay) of the Empress Formation were deposited on the floors and terraces of these preglacial valleys

These older fluvial sediments were later covered by glacial till and other more recent deposits. The valleys are thus called *buried valleys,* and the fluvial sediments within them now constitute buried-valley aquifers. The drainage pattern of these buried valleys is shown in Figure 16.

These buried-valley aquifers are the most important and productive aquifers of the Edmonton region. The larger buried valleys, such as the Beverly, Onoway and Stony Valleys, can produce water at rates in excess of 8 l/s in many places. The town of Stony Plain has to pump water from an aquifer in the Beverly Valley in order to lower the water table and permit local sewer construction. As much as 30 l/s have been pumped continuously from this aquifer for more than 15 years.

The smaller tributary buried valleys, such as the Bretona, Boag, and Ardrossan Valleys, which contain proportionately less coarse gravel, produce groundwater at somewhat lower rates. These buried tributary valley aquifers are capable of producing from about 0.4 to 2 l/s.

Within the overlying glacial deposits, the groundwater picture is in great contrast. The glacial deposits primarily consist of till, which has very low permeability and in which groundwater moves slowly, at rates of only a few to tens of centimetres per year. However, local lenses and small channels of sand or gravelly sand are found within the tills. These sands were deposited by meltwater streams from the melting ice sheet. In the Edmonton region, numerous shallow wells draw their water supplies from these sand and gravel lenses. The production capability of these wells is generally low, because the lenses of sand and gravel are of limited size. Short-term supplies from such wells are generally suitable for domestic purposes only, but even so, water shortages arise. Water pumped from the small permeable lenses can be depleted by over-pumping, and it can only be replenished by water moving through the relatively impermeable till. To circumvent this problem, wells that are drilled in till are generally of large diameter and hence have a large storage capacity within the well bore.

In some parts of the Edmonton region, the glacial till is capped by dune sands, deposited by storm winds blowing across the barren landscape after the retreat of the last glacier. Large fields of such post-glacial sand dunes are situated north of Devon, north of Bruderheim, and near Redwater. Some shallow water wells have been completed in these dune deposits. However, because the sands are highly permeable and are at the ground surface, they are particularly prone to contamination from septic systems or farmyard wastes and can quickly become unsuitable for a domestic water supply.

The chemistry of the groundwater in glacial deposits in the Edmonton region differs significantly from that of the waters in the underlying bedrock. The most notable difference is that water in glacial deposits is generally hard because of its high calcium and magnesium content, whereas that from bedrock is soft, having a high sodium content. Water from glacial deposits generally has a high iron content, and iron removal is required to make the water suitable for household use. The chemical quality of water from glacial deposits also differs over short distances, reflecting the more local nature of the groundwater flow systems as compared to bedrock water. The TDS content of glacial-deposit water generally ranges from less than 500 to more than 3000 mg/l and exceeds 6000 mg/l in some places. Water from wells completed in dune sand and in some parts of the main buried-valley aquifers has a TDS content of less than 500 mg/l and is of the calcium, magnesium bicarbonate type. Salinities in excess of 1500 mg/l are generally associated with high sulphate content. This type of water is typically found in local sand lenses within till and within the smaller, buried tributary valley aquifers such as the Boag and Ardrossan Valleys.

■ Local Groundwater Features

We have already learned that groundwater is in constant motion in the saturated subsurface, and that this movement is down-gradient, i.e. from high to low water table elevations. At any point in the saturated subsurface, groundwater has an energy level represented by the elevation to which water rises in a well completed at that point. This well-water elevation is known as the *hydraulic head*. It has two components: 1. the *pressure-head* component which is represented by the height of the water column above the point; and 2. *the elevation* of the point above some datum, generally taken as sea level. At the water table, the pressure head is zero (i.e. the water is at atmospheric pressure) and the hydraulic head is equivalent to the elevation of the water table.

The differences in hydraulic head from one place to another are primarily generated by differences in the water table elevation. Whereas the *depth to* the water table ranges from zero to a few metres below ground surface in the Edmonton region, *the elevation of the water table* differs considerably from place to place. For example, the water table elevation beneath the topographically high Cooking Lake Moraine is about 150 m higher than that in the North Saskatchewan River valley. It is this difference in water table elevation that is the driving force to move groundwater from the upland toward the river valley. Thus, like surface water, groundwater flows from uplands, such as the Cooking Lake Moraine, toward topographically lower areas. Along the flow paths, the energy level is dissipated by friction.

A second important consideration pertaining to movement of groundwater is the permeability of the rock media through which it moves. Groundwater flow directions are refracted, or bent, as water moves from relatively low permeability materials into aquifers, the amount of refraction being proportional to the permeability contrast, or difference. In this sense, the direction of groundwater flow is locally modified by the more permeable beds. In general, water flows toward material of high permeability and is then concentrated within and along the more permeable zone.

The general pattern of groundwater flow is thus downward flow beneath uplands, upward flow beneath lowlands, and lateral flow beneath the intervening slopes. This general flow pattern is locally modified by refraction and the concentration of flow within the highly permeable zones.

The above conditions result in a variety of interesting phenomena related to groundwater conditions. For example, the loss of hydraulic head that is required to drive groundwater movement manifests itself as follows.

Beneath upland areas, where groundwater moves downward, the head loss results in lower heads in successively lower aquifers. That is, at any one point, the elevation to which water rises in wells is lower in the deeper aquifers. For two wells drilled at the same point, but finished in two different aquifers, the water level is shallow for the shallow aquifer and deeper for the deeper aquifer.

In lowland areas, where groundwater movement is toward the ground surface, the opposite is true. Water levels are higher as successively deeper aquifers are tapped. This condition may progress to the point where the hydraulic head is actually above the ground surface for the deeper aquifers. The resulting groundwater phenomenon is a *flowing well*. It is worthy of note that the high hydraulic head associated with such flowing wells is in response to a high elevation of the water table beneath an upland, which might be many kilometres away. The modifying effect of contrast in permeability between adjacent strata is demonstrated in the Edmonton region in several ways. First, whereas groundwater flow is from uplands toward lowlands, the flow is also noticeably directed toward the highly permeable buried-valley aquifers. Within the buried-valley aquifers flow is from higher toward lower elevation.

Second, areas of flowing wells are generally located where bedrock aquifers subcrop at relatively low elevations (Figure 16). For example, areas of flowing wells 3 to 15 km southeast of Lamont are related to the subcrop of the Lower Birch Lake Member. Numerous flowing wells along the northwest, east and southeast parts of the Cooking Lake Moraine are related to the subcrop of coal seams in the lower part of the Horseshoe Canyon Formation. A third group of flowing wells to the east and west of Kavanagh (near Leduc) are associated with the zone of fractured permeable sandstone in the upper part of the Horseshoe Canyon Formation.

Third, the areas of flowing wells along the flanks of the Cooking Lake Moraine upland are also characterized by numerous small springs and seeps (Figure 16). These are typical "contact" springs, resulting from groundwater discharge from fractured coal seams in contact and underlain by impervious shale. Such springs are located along a curved line extending to 17 km south of Tofield; 11 km east of Ardrossan (just east of Bennett Lake); and 3 to 5 km

north of Ardrossan (along Pointe Aux Pins Creek).

Some of the springs in the Pointe Aux Pins Basin produce "soap holes", which represent an interesting groundwater phenomenon. Particularly well-developed examples are located in the NE 1/4, Section 22, Township 53, Range 22. Soap hole springs or seeps are characterized by soft, quaky ground surrounding a central core of cohesionless mud with groundwater discharge. The centre part is in a "quick" state, much as in *quicksand*. It is possible to insert a 3 to 4 m pole vertically into the central part, and numerous visitors can attest to the "quick" nature, having ventured slightly too close to the centre.

■ **Water Witchers – Diviners – Hydrogeologists**

The Edmonton region is relatively rich in groundwater and virtually anyone who drills a well has a fair chance of finding water. A random choice of a drill site, using the non-scientific approach of a "witcher" or a "diviner" might not guarantee the correct choice of aquifer. A number of aquifers, we now know, may occur below any given site. Depending upon the choice of aquifer, the drill exploration may fail to get a good, reliable supply of water or may produce a quality of water which is unusable. This is where the skills of the hydrogeologist can be applied, using scientific data to help in the proper location and depth estimation for the well. In other words, the non-scientific approach may find water, but will it be usable water and will there be enough to last?

Soils

Steven Pawluk

The soils upon which we walk, grow our food and build our shelters form a sensitive envelope of life across the land surface of the Earth. The soil body is a product of nature, derived from the action of environmental forces upon the upper surface of the Earth's crust over long periods of geological time. For example, the Black soils that formed under the cool Boreal climate and Aspen Parkland vegetation of the northern Canadian Plains are very different from the Brown soils of the southern Plains. These soils in turn are very different from the soils of the hot tropical regions. Local variations in microclimates can also result from variations in relief. As can be observed along the North Saskatchewan River valley, the north-facing slopes receive less of the sun's radiation than the south-facing slopes. The north-facing slopes are cooler and covered by forest vegetation more typical of northern regions while the south-facing slopes, being warmer and drier, are covered by grasses more typical of regions in the south of the Province. Whereas soils on these slopes have many characteristics in common with their counterparts in the respective regions to the north and south, they are younger and therefore less well developed.

Depressions, too, have a unique set of microclimatic conditions that give rise to a different set of soil characteristics and properties. Ponded water in the depressions may cause deep leaching of soils where the water table is low. Unleached soils are found in depressions where the water table is near the surface. In both instances, the soils have a pallid appearance with rusty blotches and usually a peaty surface. Soil properties are also strongly influenced by the surficial geological materials from which they form. Some soils are considered 'light' in that they are sandy in texture, whereas others are 'heavy', reflecting a largely clay content. Soils may also inherit lime and alkali salts from their parent materials. Thus, even though the regional influence of a Boreal climate and Aspen Parkland vegetation is relatively uniform for the Edmonton region, local variations in relief and surficial geological material give rise to many different kinds of soil.

Edmonton lies at the northern fringe of the Black Soil Zone where productive lands support a highly successful agricultural industry. The richness of the black top soil is a characteristic acquired through the action of living organisms on the geological materials near the land surface. The deep root systems of the tall grasses and forbs that make up the Aspen Parkland plant communities add large amounts of organic matter to the surface soil, where it is continuously altered to humus by living soil micro-organisms. The humus is incorporated within the mineral material to form highly fertile, granular and friable soils. The mineral constituents are inherited from the geological materials from which the soil forms and their composition has a strong influence on the properties of the soil.

Edmonton and much of the adjacent area lie in the relatively flat basin of Glacial Lake Edmonton, where the fine textured glaciolacustrine sediments are reflected in the high clay content of the soils. As a consequence, the wet soils compact easily when trampled and can become exceedingly hard when dry. This has been a common problem when managing these soils for lawns and gardens. The soils in the uplands are generally well drained, have relatively thick humus-rich surface horizons underlain by friable mineral subsurface horizons and are classified as **Black Chernozemic** soils. The lower-lying areas also have surface horizons rich in humus and in some locations are covered with a thin layer of peat. The subsoil however is often wet and sticky and has drab rusty grey colours. Soils in these poorer drained locations are called **Humic Gleysols.** Under careful management and with their inherent high fertility, the Black Chernozemic and Humic Gleysolic soils can yield excellent crops of wheat, oats, barley and canola. The yellow fields of canola are a common sight outside the city. Black Chernozemic soils are also developed in the rolling hills to the west of Spruce Grove. However, the high silt content and the steepness of the slopes in these pitted deltaic deposits make the soils very susceptible to erosion. Therefore, the land in this region is used mostly for pasture and forage production. The fibrous root systems of the grasses hold the soil particles together and retard erosion.

Driving south of Edmonton on Highway 2 near Nisku, we pass through scablands adjacent to Blackmud Creek where weathered Cretaceous sandy shales are exposed at or near the surface. Their brackish water origin left these bedrock materials with high concentrations of alkali salts in which sodium ions dominate. The sodium causes the clay in the subsoil to disperse and become very sticky and gooey when wet. The low strength and stickiness make it difficult to move heavy equipment across these lands after heavy rains and explains why local people commonly refer to these soils as *gumbo*. The gumbo forms a hard clay pan when dry and when the top soil is removed the subsoil often resembles a pan of buns with rounded tops. The hardness of the pan makes it difficult for plant roots to penetrate the lower layers of soil and they become rootbound. These soils are referred to as **Black Solonetz**, a word derived from the Russian literature where similar soils were first described. Solonetz soils can also be seen east of the Namao airport and elsewhere in patches within the basin of Glacial Lake Edmonton, where they develop from glaciolacustrine sediments. However, the sodium responsible for the development of these soils is derived from alkali salts brought to the surface by rising groundwater and concentrated through evaporation. As a result of the poor physical condition of the subsurface soil and the presence of alkali salts these lands are difficult to till and are typically left as pasture. The alkali salts can also be a problem for construction if these lands are used for urban development. The alkali salts corrode concrete and cause failure in foundations.

Travelling eastward from the City along Highways 14 and 16 (Figure 12) we rise in elevation leaving the basin of Glacial Lake Edmonton, and enter the Cooking Lake Moraine. Parkland vegetation gives way to Aspen Woodland. Under the closed aspen canopy in the uplands there is little ground cover and most of the organic matter added to the soil falls to the surface as leaf litter. The organic matter is rapidly devoured by the soil organisms and very little humus is added to the soil. The surface soil layers are leached of clay and take on an ashy grey colour. Hence we call these soils *Grey Luvisols*. Grey Luvisolic soils extend throughout the rolling lands of the Cooking Lake Moraine, and where these soils are cultivated the land surface has a light brownish-grey appearance. Although there is a lower clay content in the glacial till compared to the glaciolacustrine clays in the Glacial Lake Edmonton basin, these soils also compact easily and form hard surface crusts upon drying, because of their low organic matter content. The silty nature and low organic matter leave the surface soil highly susceptible to erosion and therefore these lands are often used for pasture and recreation.

Organic soils can also be seen in many of the peat bogs in and adjacent to Edmonton. Moss bogs occupy many of the poorly drained depressions in the Cooking Lake Moraine and extend throughout a large area of northwest Edmonton within and adjacent to Big Lake. West Jasper Place is constructed on land that previously was a large peat bog, where market gardens were numerous. Organic soils and alluvial soils in terraces and flood plains of the river valley are well suited for vegetable crops and at one time were used almost entirely for this purpose. Travelling along the terraces east of the City, you will see that this is still the favoured location for market gardens. However the best sites have lost out to urban sprawl and golf courses.

Archaeology

Milton Wright

Immediately prior to human settlement, Edmonton was the scene of radical environmental changes, punctuated by the monumental events of a retreating ice sheet, formation of immense glacial lake basins, and the beginnings of regional drainage systems and new plant communities. Eventually, flowing waters established a channel and began the process of entrenching itself into the loose sand and gravel sediments. No one can ever be sure when the first people arrived upon this scene, but archaeological evidence suggests that people began visiting the Edmonton region around 13,000 years ago. Evidence of these early prehistoric campsites is elusive, but archaeologists have discovered distinctive stone tools showing that temporary encampments were established along the newly formed river valley terraces by 9000 to 10,000 years ago. Both the ancient and relatively recent sites of human habitation are found along the valley margins and on the terraces of the North Saskatchewan River, demonstrating that the river valley resources have always attracted human groups.

River valleys are uniquely equipped to attract human settlement because they contain an abundance of food and material resources. Some of these resource extraction activities can be recognized in the kinds of remains preserved at archaeological sites, including bone fragments, ancient fireplaces and evidence of temporary shelters. However, the most common remains are the thousands of small stone chips left from tool making, and the fewer fragments of the manufactured stone tools themselves; both kinds of remains are the garbage of the former campsite users. In fact, the most ancient and the most recent human exploitation of the North Saskatchewan River valley are founded on the same resource: the sand and gravel deposits of the Empress Formation.

It may seem unusual for prehistoric people to have exploited a gravel deposit, but it makes perfect sense if your tool kit is based upon modified stone cobbles and pebbles. The Empress Formation contains abundant quartzite cobbles and chert pebbles. Through a process of trial and error,

early man recognized that a variety of useful and durable cutting tools could be fashioned from these materials. A quartzite cobble could be employed as a hammer stone, which would be used to fracture smaller quartzite and chert pebbles. Because of their physical properties, chert and quartzite break in a predictable fashion, allowing stone pebbles to be shaped into sharp-edged projectile points, scrapers, knives and other useful tools.

The technology required to modify stones into tools evolved over a few million years, and the skills required were likely learned by a process of observation and apprenticeship. There is a specialized stone tool technology, called bipolar technology, for processing materials like those from the Empress Formation. Normally, raw stone pebbles and cobbles would be held in the hand, while a heavy quartzite hammer stone would be used to fracture the piece and fashion the sharp durable cutting edge. However, sometimes the raw material is too small for easy hand holding. The prehistoric stone tool specialists found that, by placing the small pebble on an anvil and striking the piece with the hammerstone, they could successfully detach useable flakes, and modify the original pebble in such a way that it could be used as a tool. Most archaeological sites in the Edmonton area contain evidence of this bipolar technology showing that people were attracted to the region, because of both food resources and non-edible resources that could be used to manufacture tools.

The permanent settlement of the

Edmonton region became a reality in the late 18th century, with the establishment of fur trade posts along the North Saskatchewan River. The Hudson's Bay Company, The North West Company and the X.Y. Company all established posts along the river, but it was the Hudson's Bay Fort Edmonton posts which figured most strongly. A replica of Fort Edmonton has been reconstructed upriver from the Quesnell Bridge and provides public interpretation for the fur trade era, but there is no longer any surface evidence of the posts located near the Rossdale Power Plant or on the Legislature grounds (excavation of this latter post is yielding valuable data). These fur trade posts were well situated to take advantage of the transportation facility provided by the North Saskatchewan River. Fort Edmonton quickly became the hub for a trading network that channelled the flow of furs and other goods downriver from the surrounding territories. Inland trading networks often took advantage of natural landscape features, such as prominent linear structures like the glacial spillway channel that provided the basis for the Athabasca Landing fur trade route.

The fur trade posts soon resulted in seasonal settlement by native peoples, and the river flats by the present Rossdale Power Plant and the Victoria Golf Course were the scene of large encampments during the conduct of the trading transactions. This seasonal settlement was soon expanded to the point of becoming casual settlement and finally permanent settlement by a diverse array of immigrant populations. The majority of this settlement was situated on higher ground, with the river flats continuing to serve as casual encampment areas until the early 1900s. The fur trade resulted in fundamental changes in the way the native people utilized the resources of the North Saskatchewan River valley, and irrevocably altered the course of 10,000 years of human adaptation to the resources and landscape features of the region.

The use of the river valley by the fur trade set the stage for the later development of the river valley resources, which saw a variety of resource extraction enterprises including brick-making, coal mining and placer gold dredging. These enterprises relied on the transportation facility provided by the river, and ferry transport was an important component in the economic development of the Edmonton region. Little physical evidence remains of these various river valley industries, but old photographs provide a glimpse into the hustle and bustle that characterized the river valley during the turn of the century. Many of the historic trails established during the fur trade became the cart tracks and ultimately the roadways of the 20th century. The increasing demand for year-round reliable transportation access saw Edmonton's river fords and ferry boat crossings converted to bridges.

3 WEALTH FROM THE GROUND

Gold That Glitters

Roger D. Morton and Ronald Mussieux

■ The Edmonton Gold Rush – A Past Era

Edmonton annually celebrates its connection with the overland route to the Klondike gold rush of 1898 as though this was the true beginning of its historical association with the precious metal. But the Edmonton area had already been a gold-mining centre for some forty years by the time the Klondike fields were discovered!

Placer gold has been mined in the Edmonton region for the past 130 years and the metal played an important role in the early evolution from a fur-trading station into a thriving urban community. Most people outside Alberta are unaware of the amount of gold which lies scattered across the surface of the Province, and most visitors are surprised when told that anyone can walk down to the banks of the North Saskatchewan River and still pan visible gold and platinum.

Today, there are no major gold mining activities on the rivers of Alberta because the low concentrations of gold are insufficient to support a commercial operation. Government regulations also now prevent large-scale placer mining operations on the rivers in order to protect the drainage systems and river banks from environmental damage.

The only placer activity to be observed along the rivers now is the occasional "weekend hobby" miner with a tiny sluice box or gold pan. Probably the greatest benefit is from the fresh air experience rather than from the amount of gold which they recover!

The story begins when, with the decline of the California gold rush in 1853, thousands of gold-hungry miners dispersed and left for the reportedly richer goldfields of Nevada, Arizona, New Zealand and Australia. Many of the prospectors drifted north, discovering new gold occurrences throughout the northwest U.S.A. In 1857 they stumbled across the placer gold of the Fraser River in British Columbia and in 1860 they found the rich Cariboo goldfields. By 1863 they had discovered gold in the East Kootenay Range of British Columbia, around Wild Horse Creek. It was men travelling to and from these workings in British Columbia via Fort Edmonton who first panned gold from the gravels of the North Saskatchewan River.

■ The Early Days (1859 - 1895)

In 1859, Dr. James Hector of the Palliser Expedition was shown samples of gold washed from gravels in the Fort Edmonton area. The discovery had been made by prospectors on their way west from Minnesota to the Fraser River goldfields. By 1862, news of the Fort Edmonton discovery had reached the Fraser River area and a group of miners, including Thomas Clover, crossed the Rocky Mountains via the Yellowhead Pass to reach Fort Edmonton. Thomas Clover and his associates mined in the North Saskatchewan River valley for a number of years, and his name is perpetuated in the districts of Cloverdale and Clover Bar. In 1862, a group of 175 prospectors from eastern Canada, known as the Overlanders, travelled to Fort Edmonton, en route to the Cariboo goldfields of British Columbia. Of these adventurers, sixty remained in the Edmonton area to try their luck in the alluvial gravels of the North Saskatchewan River.

News of the Edmonton discoveries reached the disillusioned miners of the declining East Kootenay goldfields, and soon a party of prospectors was wending its way through the Kicking Horse Pass to seek fortune in Fort Edmonton. Among these newcomers were James Gibbons and Sam Livingstone. Gibbons, the inventor of the "grizzly" mining method and an important source of recorded information for the period, was experienced in placer mining in both California and the Fraser River area. Gibbons spent the years working the gravels of the North Saskatchewan River between Big Island and Fort Saskatchewan. He later settled with other prospectors on Miner's Flat, which is the present-day Laurier Park. Gibbons claimed that he was able to

Sir James Hector (1834-1907)

James Hector was the geologist and surgeon of the Palliser Expedition, the first major scientific expedition to study the Plains and Rocky Mountain regions of Western Canada. Hector was born and educated in Edinburgh, Scotland, graduating in medicine with a strong background in geology, botany and chemistry.

Between 1857 and 1860, the Palliser Expedition explored the vast country between Red River Settlement (Winnipeg) and Vancouver Island. Hector recognized Cretaceous and Tertiary strata, and was the first to describe the three erosional levels of the Plains. In addition to recognizing the coal and clay resources of the Fort Edmonton area, Hector's report was the first to note that gold was being recovered from the North Saskatchewan River. Searching for a rail route through the Rockies, Hector sketched their general structure and named several mountains. The name of the Kicking Horse Pass commemorates an accident in which Hector was kicked and knocked unconscious by one of his packhorses.

Hector provided medical assistance to the aboriginal people, gaining their respect and contributing greatly to the overall acceptance of the Expedition.

After leaving Canada, Hector settled in New Zealand, becoming the first Director of that country's Geological Survey in 1865. He was knighted in 1887.

Photo credit: Glenbow Archives

produce an average of 0.8 ounces of gold per day between spring break-up and fall freeze-up. He noted that the gravel bars were most productive at low-water periods following floods.

Other miners claimed that they could recover 0.5 ounces per day during the low water months of May, September and October. During the high water period of June to August the miners could produce no more than 0.05 to 0.06 ounces per day.

The first miners of the Edmonton area used either pans or "grizzlies". A grizzly is a device to separate fine-grained materials from coarser fractions such as boulders. In the case of the grizzlies used in this district it was necessary for the miners to separate the finer sand fraction because it was this sand which contained the small flakes of gold. No larger nuggets are ever found in these gravels. The grizzly, shown in Figure 17 , was the

standard device used in the early days. Gravel placed in the dump box was washed with water onto the apex of the grizzly bar set. Larger rocks then tumbled down either side of the grizzly, while finer gravel and sand dropped down into the sluice box. The bottom of the sluice box was lined by a coarse wool blanket which caught the fine black sand with gold and platinum grains. At regular intervals the blanket was taken out and washed in a tub (the launder). The gold-bearing black sand was then taken from the launder, and panned to concentrate the gold. Because it is almost impossible to separate physically the gold from all the black sand, the final extraction of the gold was done by amalgamation

Provincial Archives of Alberta B.5235

Figure 17. A placer gold miner using a portable grizzly on a gravel bar of the North Saskatchewan River in what is now central Edmonton. The upper dump box has been modified into a wheelbarrow, allowing the miner to quarry gravel some distance from the water's edge. The pail has been fitted with a long handle to ease the effort of supplying water to the dump box (1895).

with mercury. In this process mercury dissolves the gold and an amalgam (alloy) cake is formed. When the amalgam is heated, the mercury distills off and a spongy mass of gold is left behind.

The grizzly method of gold recovery is still popular among hobby placer miners on the North Saskatchewan River today. Over time little of the design has changed, except that the sluice boxes are now plastic or aluminum and the wool blanket has been replaced by ribbed rubber matting or indoor-outdoor carpeting. There are also legal limits on the dimensions of the system, the rate of water throughput and the use of mercury is illegal. These requirements are defined in the Government of Alberta placer mining act.

■ The Boom Era (1895 - 1907)

The peak of gold mining in the Edmonton district was reached in the period between 1895 and 1907. According to Dr. G.M. Dawson of the Geological Survey of Canada, who visited the goldfields in 1895 and 1898, the principal "paying bars" at that time extended about 100 km upstream and 100 km downstream from Edmonton. At that time he estimated that some 300 miners were working in the North Saskatchewan River valley.

After the initial success of small-scale mining in the banks and exposed bars of the North Saskatchewan River, it was inevitable that entrepreneurial activity would increase and that expertise would be brought to the area by people who had worked in other gold districts.

George Mercer Dawson (1849-1901)

G.M. Dawson is considered one of Canada's greatest scientists, not only for his contributions to geology but also for his work in ethnology and archaeology. Dawson was born in Pictou, Nova Scotia, and educated at McGill University and the Royal School of Mines, London, England.

Childhood illness left Dawson with severe physical handicaps. He was a hunchback, under 1.5 m in height and suffered lung problems. However, there was not a tougher, more capable field geologist in Canada. In 1873, Dawson was appointed geologist and botanist to the British North American Boundary Commission, whose purpose was to survey and mark the 49th parallel of latitude from Lake of the Woods to the Rocky Mountains. During this survey, in 1874, Dawson made the first discovery of dinosaur bones in Canada, near Wood Mountain, Saskatchewan. In 1875 he joined the Geological Survey of Canada and for the next 20 years spent nearly every field season investigating the geology of the Cordillera, including the Rocky Mountains, the British Columbia Interior and the southern Yukon. In 1895 Dawson became Director of the Geological Survey of Canada and remained in that office until his death from a sudden illness in 1901. As Director, Dawson continued to do fieldwork and in 1898 he spent part of the summer in Edmonton studying gold dredging on the North Saskatchewan River.

Dawson's contributions to ethnology include his classic report on the Haida Indians of the Queen Charlotte Islands, and a collection of native artifacts from his travels that laid the foundation of the ethnological collection of the National Museum of Canada (now the Canadian Museum of Civilization). Both Dawson City, Yukon, and Dawson Creek, B.C., were named after him.

It was in the early 1890s that dredges first began to exploit the submerged sectors of bars and the mid-stream portion of the North Saskatchewan River. The first dredges were built and operated by local entrepreneurs. They were known as "dippers" or "spoon dredges" and were essentially barge-mounted backhoes which excavated gravels in shallow water (Figure 18). The gravel was then dumped into a "truck", a wagon on wheels, which was used to feed sluice boxes on the barge. The Jenner dredge and the Brindley dredge were of this dipper-type. Such dredges could recover up to 0.6 ounces of gold per day.

By 1895, American and British investments sponsored the construction of much larger, steam-powered dredges on the river (Figure 19). A steam-powered dipper-type dredge, operated by the Loveland Brothers in 1898, was recovering 1.25 to 2.0 ounces of gold per day from the North Saskatchewan River channel. In the same year, Saskatchewan Gold and Platinum Proprietary Limited operated the first bucket-wheel conveyor-type dredge on the river (Figure 20). This unit could process 2400 m³ of gravel each 24 hours; which was approximately five times the throughput capacity of the Jenner's dipper-type dredge.

But the economic viability of such dredging operations was marginal. The number of dredges decreased from twelve in 1898 to one in 1907. The highest production of gold from the North Saskatchewan River was seen

Provincial Archives of Alberta B.5332

Figure 18. A dipper-type dredge, owned by Mr. Brindley, operating in the Edmonton area. A man can be seen operating the hand-powered dipper. Gravel lifted by the dipper is loaded into a wheeled truck, which is then winched to the top of the dredge and dumped into the sluice box. Note also the coal mine across the valley behind the dredge (1894).

between 1895 and 1897 when the combined grizzly and dredge operations produced a total of 7500 troy ounces of gold. That gold would be worth around $3 million at today's prices. But by 1898, the Edmonton Gold Rush was overshadowed by the Klondike Gold Rush and many of the miners left to seek their fortune in Yukon. In 1898, the annual gold production dropped to 1200 ounces.

■ Recent Years (1907 - 1993)

Since the days of the Edmonton Gold Rush small-scale mining has been a perennial activity along many of Alberta's rivers. During the Great Depression of the 1930s, local miners could on occasion make $30 per day. But the average production during that time was probably nearer $6 per day.

Only in the years 1978 - 1981 did the region experience a resurgence of gold production. This was due to a dramatic increase in the price of gold, which sparked interest among the land-based gravel operators around Villeneuve. On the basis of this price increase, such gravel and sand operations increased the rather low efficiency of their gold

Provincial Archives of Alberta B.5327

Figure 19. A four-sluice, steam-powered (suction?) dredge on the North Saskatchewan River in the early 1900s. These mechanically powered dredges with multiple sluices could process more gravel and recover more gold than the small, hand-powered dipper-type dredges (no date).

Figure 20. The conveyor-type bucket wheel dredge operated by the Saskatchewan Gold and Platinum Proprietary Limited in the early 1900s. The buckets carried the gravel to the top of the dredge where it was washed and screened in an inclined, revolving, perforated drum called a trommel. The coarse gravel passed through the trommel and was dumped overboard at the stern of the dredge. The fine-grained materials containing the placer gold passed through the perforations in the trommel and directly into long sluice boxes (no date).

recovery circuits and thus produced more gold (and platinum). As a result the production of gold has stayed at a high level since 1981.

◼ Gold Production in Alberta (1887 - 1991)

Although placer gold has been produced in the Edmonton area since 1859, production statistics were only kept from 1887. The graph in Figure 21 shows the data for gold production in Alberta between 1887 and 1991 based on production figures obtained from

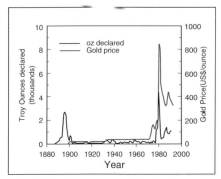

Figure 21. Placer gold production for Alberta during the period 1887-1991.

Provincial Government sources. It should be remembered, however, that such figures will constitute underestimates where production is not declared, for example to avoid payment of royalties and taxes. It is clear that few, if any, of the small-scale placer mining operations recorded their production with the authorities. However, the figures offer a fascinating insight into the economic incentive for mining placer gold in this region.

Figure 21 shows that the gold-mining activity of Alberta has, during the past 100 years, been very much a function of the international price of gold and of global economic factors. Whenever the price of gold has risen on the international market there has been an immediate resurgence in gold production in Alberta. Such upward price changes took place in 1934 and 1974 through 1980. The Great Depression of 1929 - 1941 is clearly reflected in the rate of Albertan gold production, for at that time the local populace would be desperate to earn money in any legal way possible. There are many local stories of fathers and grandfathers who took pick and shovel down into Alberta's river valleys to dig for gold during the depression years. Also during times of major wars (e.g. World War I (1914 - 18), the Korean War (1950 - 53) and the Vietnam War (1957 - 75), the Albertan gold miners were more active, striving to supplement earnings. It is noteworthy that the production figures during World War II (1939 - 45) actually show a reduction in mining activity. Probably due to the fact that many able-bodied men were on duty in the armed forces, and the whole of Canadian society was engaged in the national war effort.

■ The Gold-(Platinum) Deposits

The gold-(platinum) deposits of the Edmonton region are of the type referred to as placer and paleoplacer deposits. The term "gold-(platinum)" deposits infers that they contain only a minor portion of platinum relative to gold. The maximum amount of platinum, and therefore minimum ratio of platinum:gold, is around 1:20.

Placer deposits in the Edmonton region are unconsolidated alluvial deposits of sand and gravel deposited by both modern and ancient rivers. Because gold and platinum are heavy minerals (specific gravity = 19.3 and 21.4, respectively) they quickly sink in water (specific gravity = 1.0) along with other heavy minerals (e.g. magnetite, garnet, zircon). Together with the predominant magnetite fraction, gold and platinum constitute components of "black sands". Black sands are either natural concentrations or man-made concentrates of the heavy minerals of sediments.

The natural concentration of black sands happens wherever the velocity of the river is significantly reduced, for example, where a river widens and where meanders develop. There is a marked contrast in flow velocity across a meander, with the water moving slowly on the inside of the curve and flowing more rapidly in the centre (the thalweg) of the river and on the outside of the meander curve. The flow velocity is also affected by the development of channel bars in a river. Because of this, it is commonplace to find richer gold-(platinum) concentrations in point bars on the inside of meanders and in the mid-channel bars. This concept is demonstrated by the fact that most hobby gold miners in Edmonton can be seen today on the point bar which occurs just to the east of the Groat Bridge, below Emily Murphy Park. In the past, mining took place at such places as "the Big Bend" and "Clover Bar". The names of both of these localities bear witness to the importance of meanders and river bars in the concentration of placer gold and platinum.

The modern placer gold-(platinum) deposits of the Edmonton region are also known as "skim gold-(platinum) deposits" or as "flood gold-(platinum) deposits". Concentrations are typically lower in bulk samples taken from excavations at depth than those taken from the upper few centimetres of a recently exposed alluvial bar in the modern river. The gold and platinum are typically concentrated at times of flood and left stranded on the surface of river bars. Thus, a post-flood or post-spring thaw period is the time when the most gold and platinum is recoverable from sluicing or panning operations on the modern rivers.

Paleoplacer gold-(platinum) deposits are represented by what are thought to be preglacial (Empress Formation) or interglacial alluvial gravels. These gravels occur in several areas around Edmonton e.g. Villeneuve, Entwhistle and Heatherdown. The gravel deposits are the remains of the bar systems developed in a network of former rivers which flowed across the plains

before the last Pleistocene glaciation. Even in 1898, small-scale mining operations were recovering gold from these gravels, which were exposed along the banks of the North Saskatchewan River. For the past thirty years, bulk gravel-, sand- and aggregate-producers in this area of Alberta have been producing gold and platinum as a by-product of their operations. Indeed, probably most of the gold production declared to the government in recent years came from such paleoplacer production. The production figures cannot be used to estimate the grades of the paleoplacer deposits in the region, because the recovery processes used during gravel- and sand-washing operations are notoriously inefficient.

■ Nature of the Gold and Platinum

The placer gold and platinum found in the Edmonton region are classified as "flour" gold and "flour" platinum. The precious metals do not occur as large nuggets which can be picked up and handled, but as tiny flakes about 0.5 to 0.1 mm in diameter and only a few hundredths of a millimetre thick. At this small grain size, the dense gold and platinum can exhibit an unique behaviour; the grains of flour gold and platinum can actually float on the surface of water! Indeed, when panning the gold and platinum in the river gravels it is generally advisable to add a little detergent to the water to break the surface tension and so allow the minute precious metal flakes to sink to the bottom of the pan, instead of floating off.

The raw gold of the Edmonton region is very pure and contains only trace quantities of silver and copper. When the grains are cut in half they reveal that they actually have an outer zone of 100% pure gold. This pure gold skin has developed because during transportation in the rivers the raw gold has been pounded underwater. This has resulted in vulnerable metals such as silver and copper being chemically leached out of the original, less-pure gold-silver-copper alloy. Gold has not been dissolved, because it is a noble (solution resistant) metal. This effect is commonly seen in natural gold alloys which have been transported, deposited and re-eroded, over a long period of time.

The platinum of the Edmonton region is actually an iron-platinum alloy known as iso-ferroplatinum. Minor traces of other platinum group elements (iridium, osmium and rhodium) also are alloyed with the platinum. The raw platinum grains, like the gold, are tiny flakes, only noticeable among the gold concentrates by their silver white colour.

■ Where Did the Gold and Platinum Originate?

The origin of the gold and platinum has intrigued geologists for many years, for in some people's eyes the answer to this riddle could well lead to the discovery of a new "motherlode". Early workers speculated that the gold must have come from the rocks of the Precambrian Shield to the northeast, the only region in Canada known to carry bedrock gold occurrences. After all, they reasoned, the glaciers of the

Pleistocene Epoch had brought down numerous rocks from the Shield into the Edmonton region. Why should the gold (and platinum) not have been a part of the glacial tills? The other possibility was that the precious metals came from eroded Cretaceous bedrock in the region. But no one had ever observed any paleoplacer concentrations of platinum or gold in rocks of Cretaceous age in this district.

The enigma remained until 1987, when gold was discovered by Mr. Kletl in the Jasper region of western Alberta. Subsequent investigation of the gold occurrence revealed that the gold occurred in small, rich veins within Lower Cambrian strata in the area of the Committee Punchbowl at the Alberta - British Columbia boundary. These basal Cambrian strata were the same rocks which had supplied the ubiquitous white quartzite pebbles and boulders (Gog quartzite) which are found in all the gold- and platinum-bearing gravels of the region. Thus the Albertan "motherlode" country lies protected in Jasper National Park.

Subsequent research suggested that the gold probably was eroded from the Cambrian bedrock during early Cretaceous time, deposited with sediments, and later (during Tertiary and Quaternary time) eroded and transported in the ancient rivers of Alberta. The final stage of re-erosion placed the gold in the alluvial sediments of today's rivers.

The origin of the platinum in Alberta's placer deposits is a little more speculative. It is likely that it too, like the gold, came from the Rocky

Mountains. The nearest bedrock which we know today to carry platinum in any concentrations is the area around Princeton, British Columbia. There, in the area of the Tulameen River, platinum occurs in an ultramafic intrusion and is abundant in local alluvial placers. This intrusion is part of a belt of ultramafic rocks which occurs sporadically through British Columbia.

This belt could have been the origin of the platinum in Alberta, which would suggest that the platinum-bearing ultramafic rocks had been eroded at a time when the Front Ranges of the Rocky Mountains were not a barrier and rivers flowed eastward from the interior region of British Columbia into Alberta.

Black Diamonds

John D. Campbell

■ Coal Mines Of Old Edmonton

It was the abundance of coal in the banks of the North Saskatchewan River that made it possible for Easterners and Europeans to establish the City of Edmonton so quickly and so successfully. The Hudson's Bay Company, with its easy access to native expertise, dug only a little coal from the bank below Fort Edmonton for the blacksmith's forge, but the settlers who came after 1870 desperately needed coal to survive in their flimsy first houses. John Walter, boat builder, lumberman and first Edmonton industrialist, imported the first coal stove to Edmonton in 1874. By then, a few settlers had begun to mine coal in earnest, and production continued without interruption within the city until the last mine closed in 1970, nearly 100 years later. Agriculture certainly inspired the Edmonton land boom, but coal made it possible.

At least 109 coal mines have operated within the City of Edmonton and the

actual number is known to be much higher. The first mines in the Canadian Prairies almost certainly were here, but official government recording only began in 1897; we know of earlier operations only from newspaper reports, advertisements and litigation records.

Nearly 90 percent of all coal mines in Edmonton were tiny, ephemeral and often dangerous, operating in winter and then closing when the seasonal demand declined. They could only afford horizontal tunnels and therefore clustered where upper coal seams were exposed in convenient river cliffs: (1) east of the Edmonton Convention Centre and Grierson Hill, around the point of land above Riverdale and Alex Taylor Road; (2) in the river cliffs below Scona Hill (99th Street) and the Old Timers' Cabin; (3) in the ravine ("Dowler's Creek", now obscured by 98th Avenue) north of the Strathearn District; and (4) in the big cliff east across the river from Rundle Park.

Locations and names of these little mines changed, resulting in utter confusion; only a few individuals such as Baldwin, Humberstone, Ottewell and Ross reappear in the records and these were more likely promoters than miners.

The little mines peaked just after 1900, then almost disappeared. As the city matured, a new class of mine appeared and for the next 70 years, just 17 moderately large, well-planned mines produced virtually all the coal in Edmonton. The first of these, the Clover Bar Mine, under the present Abbotsfield Mall in east Beverly, began in 1897; the last one, the Whitemud Creek (Red Hot) Mine by the ski-tow in Whitemud Valley, north of Whitemud Drive, closed in March 1970. The largest, longest-running mine was the Black Diamond, with a pit-head in the middle of the Strathcona Science Park; over 49 years it produced nearly 3 million tonnes, or more than 22 percent of all the coal ever mined in Edmonton.

Even these 17 larger mines had a confusion of names: there were two "Ottewell" mines and two "Bush" mines; both the Chinook and the Standard ran at different times as "City Mines"; "Pen" became "Penn", merged with Chinook, then moved out of the city. Mergers, interlocking directorships and shared management were common; some people appeared and re-appeared: Campbell, Dowdell, Fraser, McIntyre etc. and especially the irrepressible Jack Starky, founder and trader of many mines, both within and outside the city.

The map Figure 22 and Table 1 show the locations, names and some pertinent facts of the 17 bigger Edmonton mines.

Seven of these big mines had railway spurs, but the shipping trade was never significant; the main market was domestic heating in and around the city. When natural gas arrived in Edmonton from Wainwright in 1923, the coal trade began to decline; by 1953, only the Whitemud Creek Mine was left, and it closed in 1970.

■ Coal Seams

The coal seams around Edmonton are undisturbed layers of transformed plant remains up to 3 m thick, stretching many kilometres horizontally in all directions. They and the adjacent beds of sandstone and shale undulate a little, but dip on average about two metres per kilometre to the southwest.

H.H. Beach, in 1934, ascribed all coal occurrences that were mined in the city to three seams (Figure 23) which he designated Lower or No. 3; Clover Bar or No. 4 (7.5 to 12 m above No. 3); and Weaver or No. 7 (32 to 46 m above No. 4). There is disagreement over details of Beach's classification especially regarding the seven other "seams" that he recognized, but it is still useful as a general guide.

Edmonton coal is sub-bituminous in rank, i.e. one step better (as fuel) than lignite; it is low in ash and burns for a long time with a cheery, bright flame.

Of the more than 13 million tonnes produced in the century of coal mining within Edmonton, more than 95 percent came from the Clover Bar seam, which is exposed at river level

Figure 22. The 17 major historic coal mines of old Edmonton. Showing the edge of the river valley and the line of geological section A - B (see Figure 23). 1. Beverly-2. Black Diamond-3. Old Bush-4. New Bush-5. Clover Bar- 6. Dawson-7. Fraser-McKay-8. New Humberstone-9. Kent-10. Marcus- 11. New Ottewell-12. Penn, Chinook-13. Premier-14. Red Hot-15. Standard-16. Twin City-17. Whitemud Creek-18. Strathcona.

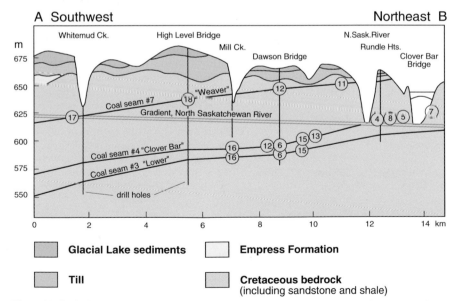

Figure 23. Geological section A - B (see map Figure 22) through the City of Edmonton. Showing the three principal commercial coal seams and major coal mines (numbers as in map and Table 1).

Table 1. Historic Major Coal Mines of Old Edmonton.

Map Location No. and Name (Figure 22)	Date Operating	Cumulative Production metric tonnes x 10^3	Comments
"Big" Mines: 10,000 tonnes annually and 100,000 tonnes cumulative			
1. Beverly	1931-51	759	Shafts 45 m deep ~42 St. and 121 Ave.
2. Black Diamond	1903-52	2896	Main slope 300 m south of Strathcona Science Park exhibits building
3. Old Bush	1904-25	491	Shaft 14 m deep, also slope; 120 m west of Rundle Park tennis courts
4. New Bush	1917-44	640	2 shafts 18 and 55 m deep and drift at north end of Rundle - Gold Bar footbridge
5. Clover Bar	1897-1923	328	Shaft 24 m deep at 118 Ave. and Victoria Trail; drifts near west end of Beverly Bridge
6. Dawson	1907-44	656	Shaft 35 m deep, east end of Dawson Bridge
7. Fraser-McKay	1904-41	1068	Shaft 30.5 m deep, S side Hwy. 16 E, 550 m SW of Alberta Research Council
8. New Humberstone	1899-1934	1166	Shaft 33 m deep, 50 m south of 111 Ave. and 30 Street
9. Kent	1933-45	524	Shaft 50 m deep in Brown & Root yard, 100 m SW Sherwood Park Fwy. CNR overpass
10. Marcus	1917-40	995	Shaft 38 m deep, south side Hwy. 16 E, 350 m south of Alberta Research Council
11. New Ottewell	1932-50	204	Shafts 13 m deep; 150 m S of 101 Ave. 190 m west of BPCO Inc. plant, west side of ravine
12. Penn, Chinook, etc.	1901-30	977	Various shafts about 20 m below river level; operated 1907-19 with convict labour
13. Premier	1920-37	233	Shaft 23 m deep, 170 m S of Concordia College at foot of hill; mine roof 12.2 m thick
14. Red Hot	1931-51	242	Slopes in ravine beside Capilano Fwy. at S end of bridge; 9 m below river
15. Standard	1906-23	336	Shaft 28 m deep in mouth of Kinnaird Ravine, slope in ravine 130 m W of 76 Street
16. Twin City	1908-21	461	Shafts 51 m deep in mouth of Mill Creek Ravine; west side of bike path at 93 Avenue
17. Whitemud Creek	1952-70	248	Slope in W wall of Whitemud Creek 200 m N of Whitemud Drive, just north of ski tow
Two Lesser Mines of Special Interest			
18. Strathcona	1905-11	71	Shafts 30 m deep in middle of Kinsmen Park Pitch & Putt
19. St. Albert	1911-16	28	Deepest shaft Levasseur Rd. and Sir W. Churchill Ave. St. Albert; an expensive 98 m failure

downstream from the Rundle - Gold Bar footbridge (see Site 8 in Chapter 5). Three mines, the Strathcona (not a big mine), the new Ottewell and the Whitemud Creek, dug all their coal from the Weaver seam, as did the Pen Mine between 1907 and 1919, when it was run with convict labour by the Edmonton Federal Penitentiary. At various times, several mines, including the Standard, Penn, Dawson and Twin City, tried to exploit the Lower seam, with little success because of unsafe conditions.

■ Mining Methods

In Edmonton, all coal was mined underground, not strip-mined; it was hauled to the surface through inclined slopes (Black Diamond Mine) or vertical shafts (Dawson Mine). The St. Albert Mine, the deepest local mine, spent a fortune to sink an oval concrete-lined shaft 98.1 m deep, and found no coal worth mining.

Mined coal seams in Edmonton were usually 1.0 to 1.5 m thick so the miners had to work on their knees. Coal was usually "trammed" in rail cars to the foot of the shaft or slope by horses, usually brawny little Welsh Ponies, although the Whitemud Mine worked a team of big Clydesdales underground until 1970. Ponies were the miners' pets, sharing their work and their lunch sandwiches. One tale is told of beloved "Shorty", whose death at 38 years was mourned publicly in Forest Heights. Nine of the big mines near the river worked at or below river level; and some possibly under the river.

Donaldson Bogart Dowling (1858-1925)

Donaldson Dowling, one of the most respected geologists of the Geological Survey of Canada, spent forty years examining the economic potential of rocks in the Great Plains and eastern Rocky Mountains. He was born in Ontario and graduated from McGill University as a gold medallist in civil engineering.

Dowling joined the Survey in 1884, first working as an assistant to J.B. Tyrrell during his surveys of northern Alberta and Manitoba. In 1903 he began investigations of the coal-bearing formations of the Rockies, soon discovering the rich deposits of the Bighorn Basin that were later taken up by Brazeau Collieries of Nordegg. At this time, Dowling also examined coal deposits on the plains and published a memoir on **The Edmonton Coal Field.** *Subsequently, Dowling became Great Plains Geologist for the Survey, directed and interpreted work supporting oil exploration in the Turner Valley Field, and his 1915 study of the Milk River Sandstone of southern Alberta showed it to be an important artesian groundwater aquifer, valuable to the local ranchers and farmers.*

Perhaps Dowling's best known contribution was his **Geology of The Southern Plains of Alberta,** *Geological Survey of Canada Memoir 93, which laid the foundation for the study of stratigraphy and structure in the region.*

The miner's constant challenge underground is to plan for a safe, orderly collapse of the roof; when the seam is removed, the roof has to fall. The oldest method of control, still one of the safest, is the room-and-pillar system; miners quickly extract a large rectangle of coal called a room, leaving walls of coal all around called pillars to take the weight; then they get out before the roof cracks at the pillar edges and crashes down. They repeat the process at regular intervals along the permanent entry-tunnel, winning 100 - 200 tonnes of coal from each room.

Several Edmonton mines, notably the Kent, used the more elaborate longwall system in which many miners working in unison cut the coal from a single straight face or wall as much as 120 m long; they allow the roof to collapse behind them parallel to the wall and a short distance out from it, leaving no pillars. But if the collapse goes faster than planned, chunks of roof rock can pin a miner to the wall.

Underground mining is always dangerous and there were a number of injuries and fatalities in Edmonton. The Lower seam was tempting but contained much dangerous methane gas. The most widely publicized catastrophe in the city was the Strathcona Mine fire of 1907 in which six miners died. Their funeral, which passed down Whyte Avenue, has been recorded on a well-known photograph.

■ Viewing

Very little remains of the Edmonton coal mines; the City and citizens seem to have been acutely embarrassed by this messy industry. Surprisingly few photographs are available of the bigger mines, although the squalid early little mines are well depicted. Strathcona Science Park preserves a few masonry remnants of the old Black Diamond service buildings, and vestiges of some entry portals on the river bank; bits of foundations and scrap metal from the Standard may be hidden in the undergrowth in Kinnaird Ravine; the room-and-pillar pattern of the Premier can be seen as gentle collapse depressions, with different shades of grass, in the 17th fairway, Highlands Golf Course, immediately along the

Figure 24a. The Dawson (coal) Mine site, west of Dawson Bridge, (pre-1930).

Figure 24b. The Dawson (coal) Mine site, west of Dawson Bridge, (1992).

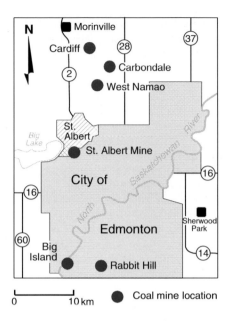

Figure 25. Areas of limited coal mining activity around Edmonton.

east side of Capilano Freeway north of the river. Mostly, however, the reclamation is complete, as the accompanying two photographs (Figure 24) of the Dawson Mine site show - the older one with shaft headframe and tipple taken before 1930 and the 1992 one with the Riverside Golf Course parking lot.

Just outside the City are five areas of lesser mining activity, shown in Figure 25; here, evidence of past industry is easier to see, especially where strip-mining occurred.

Feats Of Clay

Don Scafe

Since the first brick-making plant in Alberta opened in the Edmonton region in 1881, plants have operated at 15 localities within the current City boundaries. One plant is operating today.

In 1881, the Humberstone Brick & Coal Co. used the coal it mined east of the current Edmonton Convention Centre site as fuel to fire bricks made from river terrace clay quarried nearby. Humberstone sold the bricks for $20 per thousand; the equivalent current cost would be $560 per thousand.

James B. Little, an orphan from Ayrshire, Scotland, came to Edmonton in 1892, after learning the brick-making

business in Chicago and after making bricks in Banff for the first CPR hotel. He purchased 4 hectares of land within a few hundred metres of the Humberstone yard and started making soft mud bricks the next year. Later, an additional 8.1 hectares was purchased. Sons and grandsons have kept the business in the family. Production ceased in 1956 but the company remains a major distributor of ceramic construction products.

Two Iowa farmboys aborted their trip to the Klondike during their stop in Edmonton, after hearing of the local high-quality clays. Frank and John Pollard started making bricks by hand in 1898 on 4.25 hectares that are below and west of the south end of the High Level Bridge (CPR purchased about one third of the land from them in 1911 for their own right-of-way). With the money from the CPR purchase, new machinery was brought in from Minneapolis. Brick production ceased in 1914 when Frank joined the militia. An attempt to resume production after the war failed when the City of Edmonton foreclosed for back taxes. Many of the older brick buildings at the University of Alberta are built from bricks fired at Pollard Brothers. The Holy Trinity Anglican Church at 84th Avenue and 101st Street is built from their clinker brick. Brick rubble can be seen in the lowest river terrace bank just west of the first High Level Bridge pier.

Other brickyard operators in the first two decades of this century include P. Anderson & Co. who operated on the river flats between the current location of Muttart Conservatory and the south end of the Low Level Bridge, and the Sandison Brickyard, which became Edmonton Brick Co. Ltd., who had their plant on the river flats at the current location of Victoria Golf Course: the major dip in the seventh fairway is a remnant of the clay pit.

The largest brickyard in northern Alberta, the Acme Brick Co. Ltd., started in 1907 along the Canadian Northern Railway 10.5 km outside Edmonton; today that location is at 137th Avenue and 170th Street. Glacial Lake Edmonton clays were used to make textured, wire-cut brick by the stiff-mud process. Sewer tile, flue tile and hollow building tile also were in the product line. A 14-room bunkhouse, general store, and the proverbial Chinese cook were part of the operation. The plant was sold after World War II and resold in 1952. A tunnel dryer and kiln were added in 1954. I-XL Industries of Medicine Hat, the current owners, purchased it in 1957 and operate it as Northwest Brick & Tile. Clays from glacial lake sediments at Athabasca are used to vary the product colour selection. A major upgrade in 1982 added a new building, extruder, setting, loading, transfer equipment, dryers, kiln and holding rooms. This is the only brick plant in Alberta operating outside the Medicine Hat - Redcliff district.

To the east of the brick plant, Consolidated Concrete Ltd. has, since 1968, used the same glacial lake clays to produce a different ceramic product. "Literock", a synthetic, lightweight or "expanded" aggregate, was used for many years in the production of lightweight concrete masonry blocks, cast-in-place concrete, or precast exterior wall panels and bridge girders. Recently, its insulating properties have increased its use as a geotechnical filler material. Water and sanitation pipes do not have to be buried so deeply to be safe from freezing, and pads of this material beneath power substations provide good electrical insulation.

Clay is an industrial raw material that was prominent in the early development of Edmonton.

Gravel Bar Blues

Dixon Edwards

Many Edmontonians are aware that mineral resources are important to the economy of Alberta. But how many know that the world's two most valuable mineral resources are produced within 100 km of the City? The most valuable resource is easy to guess. It's the black liquid known as oil. The second most valuable resource may be tougher to figure out. It doesn't look valuable; in fact it's downright common. Most people live in a home that sits on it, they drive on it every day and they see tonnes of it when they look out across the City. The mineral resource is sand and gravel and its primary use is in concrete and asphalt. World-wide, sand and gravel outrank all other mineral resources in tonnage and are exceeded in value only by petroleum. It's hard to believe, but there is more money in sand and gravel than in gold or platinum or diamonds!

Sand and gravel was not always produced in the Edmonton area. We didn't begin to use it until we needed paved roads, gutter and storm water systems, concrete foundations, railway beds and paved airport runways.

The demand for sand and gravel started at the turn of the century. The first major use of sand and gravel as concrete aggregate in the City was for the High Level Bridge. Hundreds of tonnes of sand and gravel were used in its construction just before World War I and it is a testament to the longevity of concrete structures. The value of Alberta's sand and gravel production is recorded as early as 1922 when $229,091 worth was produced. The first geological information on sand and gravel resources was published by the Research Council of Alberta in 1928 by the eminent local geologist Dr. Ralph L. Rutherford.

But the heyday of sand and gravel was not in the early 1900s, it is now! The use of aggregate has grown steadily, and we use more than $130 million dollars worth each year in Alberta alone. The Edmonton Convention Centre is another monument constructed recently (Figure 26) which attests to the continued importance of sand and gravel: more than 38,000 m^3 of concrete were used in its construction.

We can only guess, but a total of about 300 million tonnes of sand and gravel have been used in the Edmonton area. Most of this was excavated from within 50 km of the City centre and much from within the City itself. One of the best records of the history of this local mining phenomenon is in the form of aerial photographs. These types of photographs have been taken of the City from as early as 1924, and they clearly show the pits that were dug in the river valley where sand and gravel was mined.

Photographs of the Mayfair Golf Course and Mayfair - Hawrelak Park area taken in 1924, 1952, 1962 and 1988 record a history which includes the development of a sand and gravel pit and its subsequent reclamation into its current land use. Figure 27 shows the

Figure 26. The Edmonton Convention Centre under construction, May 17, 1981. Massive concrete tangent piles line the walls of the building foundation.

Provincial Archives of Alberta A. 6815

area as it was in 1924. The cigar-shaped, light coloured patches are the fairways on the Mayfair Golf Course. The concentric scallop-shaped lines that run across the fairways parallel to the curved river bank are a record of the deposition of the sandy gravel point bar. Note that there is no Groat Bridge, no Provincial Museum (only Government House) and no gravel pit south of the golf course. In 1952 (Figure 28) the gravel pit has been started. Why would this gravel pit be needed? Look at this photograph. Note the new roads and homes which required sand and gravel for foundations, concrete and asphalt. In 1962 (Figure 29) the gravel pit mining is more extensive: the entire south half of the point bar looks disturbed and the Groat Bridge has

been built. In the 1988 aerial photograph (Figure 30) the gravel pit is now a park with grassy expanses and a small artificial pond. This general succession of land use: from natural condition, to sand and gravel pit, to recreational park, has been repeated many times in the City of Edmonton. Examples include Hawrelak Park, Rundle Park, Valley Zoo - Laurier Park and Hermitage Park.

There are three main geological categories of sand and gravel deposits which have supplied construction aggregate to the growing Edmonton market, these are: (1) postglacial alluvial (river valley) deposits; (2) glacial deposits; and (3) preglacial deposits. The postglacial alluvial deposits include terraces and point bars such as those at Hawrelak Park. The terraces or benches formed in the valley

Alberta Forestry, Lands and Wildlife Air Photograph C.A.74.10

Figure 27. The Mayfair Golf Course and surrounding area of the North Saskatchewan River valley - 1924. Note the scroll bars and the absence of the Groat Bridge and the Provincial Museum and the lack of a gravel pit south of the golf course.

as the river eroded by stages into the plains. These benches include sand and gravel deposited in earlier channels before the river moved sideways and began to cut downward again. Four terrace levels are identified within the valley at Edmonton (Figure 14). The Legislature Building rests on the

highest and oldest terrace, the nearby Terrace Building sits on the second oldest terrace, and John Ducey Park is on the fourth and youngest terrace. Emily Murphy Park contains the third oldest of the four terrace levels. All of these terraces were built in the last 12,000 years, since the postglacial

Aberta Forestry, Lands and Wildlife Air Photograph AS 004 #104

Figure 28. North Saskatchewan River valley - 1952.
New developments include the gravel pit south of the golf course, roads and housing.

North Saskatchewan River began to flow after melting of the continental ice sheet.

Deposits of sand and gravel formed by glacial meltwaters are called *glaciofluvial* deposits. They commonly provide useful sources of construction aggregate. The estimated occurrence and use to date of the various types of sand and gravel deposits are shown in Table 2.

Long before the advance of the continental ice sheet, rivers flowed from the Rocky Mountains across the Western Plains. In the Edmonton region about 1 km of rock was eroded by the

Figure 29. North Saskatchewan River valley - 1962.
Note enlargement of the gravel pit and construction of Groat Bridge.

Figure 30. North Saskatchewan River valley - 1988.
The gravel pit has been reclaimed and redeveloped as the municipal Hawrelak Park.

preglacial rivers. The vestiges of these ancient river channels are found at Villeneuve about 30 km northwest of Edmonton (Figure 16). Deposits of this former river supply some of the best high-quality concrete aggregate in Alberta.

Sand and gravel supplies have been building up in the Edmonton region for the last 65 million years. An estimated 500 million tonnes of usable gravel and 1800 million tonnes of sand lay within 55 km of Edmonton at the turn of the century. Since that time, one-third of a billion tonnes of sand and gravel have

Table 2. Types of Construction Sand and Gravel in Alberta, distribution of original reserves and production in Alberta for 1988.

Types of Sand and Gravel	Distribution of Reserves	Source of Production in 1988
Preglacial	20%	25%
Glacial	70%	30%
Recent alluvial	10%	45%
Total	45,000 million tonnes	42 million tonnes

been used. How much longer will these local supplies last?

Gushers and Gases

Robert E. Folinsbee

Peter Pond of the Hudson's Bay Company was the first European to recognize oil in the "tar" sands around Fort McMurray on the Athabasca River. These bitumen-bearing sands exposed along the river extend hundreds of kilometres to the southeast, and under thicker cover give way to very heavy oil at Primrose Lake and Cold Lake, and to the heavy oil at Lloydminster. These Lower Cretaceous oil deposits are now being exploited as the lighter Paleozoic oils of the Devonian and Mississippian Periods become depleted. The oil sands are by far the largest oil accumulation in North America, a giant black ace-in-the-hole for Alberta industry. The sands at Fort McMurray directly overlie porous Devonian coral reefs whose vugs are filled with a thick tarry oil. Farmers

plowing their fields around Edmonton have for a hundred years turned up giant blocks of this limestone, brought south by the ice sheets, and they regularly report to the Department of Geology at the University on their newly discovered oil fields.

It was natural, then, for the great pioneering geologist, George Mercer Dawson (of Klondike fame) to consider the oil-bearing Devonian limestone as a possible source for the oil in the bituminous sands. This origin is still argued because the oil in the great McMurray delta might equally well have been derived from life in the tropical Cretaceous seas of the Dinosaur era.

In 1894, with Edmonton as a base, Dawson recommended the drilling of two wells in his search for the great northern field (Figure 31). The first was spudded on the North Saskatchewan River, at Pakan settlement, far enough updip from the city to tap the Devonian formations at less than 900 m, the practical limit for cable tool drilling at the time. The second was located at the intersection of the Athabasca Trail from Edmonton with the Athabasca River at Athabasca Landing.

The well at Pakan missed the giant Redwater field (100 million m^3 of light Devonian crude) by 13 km, the second missed the Swan Hills field by 65 km! Oil exploration in the Edmonton area sputtered on for 50 years as action shifted to Calgary with the nearby Turner Valley anticlinal gas and oil field. Heavy oil was discovered at Wainwright and Lloydminster, and extensive natural gas fields at Viking and Kinsella. Natural gas from the Cretaceous-age Viking Formation sandstone escaped from the abandoned Pakan well (there was no Energy Resources Conservation Board then!) for half a century. Ralph Rutherford, as a student assistant in the early twenties cooked eggs over the Pakan flare for John Allan during their pioneering geological traverse from Rocky Mountain House, past Edmonton to North Battleford by river raft, complete with a tent on their "houseboat".

The Viking gas fields were tapped by further wells, and Northwestern Utilities built a pipeline that brought natural gas into Edmonton in the mid-twenties – a major engineering feat for the time. It was a single line and when it broke in mid-winter (-40°F and

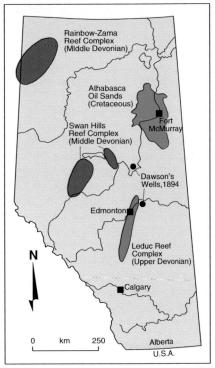

Figure 31. Middle and Upper Devonian coral reef reservoirs hold most of Canada's high-quality oil reserves, but these total only I percent of the oil in the Athabasca oil sands.

-40°C) everyone in the City of 27,000 people who had converted from coal to gas had their homes freeze up. The conservatives who had resisted the new fangled gas furnaces took in their chilled neighbours.

At about this time, Imperial Oil drilled down dip from an oil seep on the Mackenzie River at what is now Norman Wells. They found light oil in a Devonian coral reef, turning Dawson's dream of a great northern Devonian oil field into reality. Imperial (Esso) had been a principal player in discovering oil at Turner Valley, down dip from the wet gas field at the crest of the Turner Valley anticline. Thirty billion cubic metres of gas had been flared off the wet gas field during the roaring twenties and dirty thirties, finally prompting the creation of the Alberta Energy Resources Conservation Board. Thirty million cubic metres of oil were locked in the Turner Valley field by loss of pressure due to flaring. In 1946, with Turner Valley waning, the light oil situation was becoming a desperate one, with most Alberta oil brought in from Oklahoma by tank car.

At Kinsella, Imperial found a thin light-oil zone on the downdip edge of the gas field. Perhaps with Turner Valley in mind, perhaps in hope of a downdip Viking or McMurray sand field, with a distant hope of Dawson's great northern field, Imperial spudded in Leduc Number 1 in the fall of 1946. The well was located over a seismic anomaly. After oil shows in the Viking and Lower Cretaceous and a long barren journey through the D-l (the Upper Devonian Wabamun Group, Figure 32) the well (Figure 33) struck oil in the D-2, the Nisku Formation biostromal coral reef. A follow-up well failed to find oil in the Nisku biostrome but tapped a bonanza in the underlying biohermal reef, the D-3 or Leduc Formation. Other finds followed, north and south along trend. North of Leduc the Woodbend, Yekau Lake, Acheson, Big Lake, Schoep (renamed Golden Spike) and St. Albert fields created fortunes for Imperial, Chevron and

Amoco. To the southwest, due to astute leasing by Hugh Beach of the University of Alberta and Texaco, the giant fields of Wizard Lake and Bonnie Glen were brought in on Texaco land. Much of this land was freehold and great fortunes came to the farmers who had settled the land before the turn of the century, before hungry governments took over all mine and mineral rights.

The Rebus family of Leduc had an unexpected bonus thrust upon them when the Atlantic Number 3 well ran wild during the summer of 1948, creating a lake of oil on which the Rebus family held a most complicated set of royalties. The well caught fire on Labour Day, September 6, 1948. At that time I was returning from Lac de Gras, north of Yellowknife, NWT, destined to be the site of Canada's first major diamond rush (1992), at the end of the field season with the Geological Survey of Canada. I watched the great tower of smoke rise over the well as the pilot circled in amazement. This fire created an international stir second only to Saddam Hussein's 1991 action in Kuwait.

The Atlantic blowout overshadowed the discovery of Redwater in 1948 (100 million m^3 of light crude), and disappointments such as Willingdon where a giant reef had been subsequently breached by erosion and more than 100 million m^3 of oil lost.

In the years that followed, exploration farther afield brought in the Middle Devonian Swan Hills field. The elusive pinnacle reefs at Rainbow Lake and Zama, buried in salt, were discovered

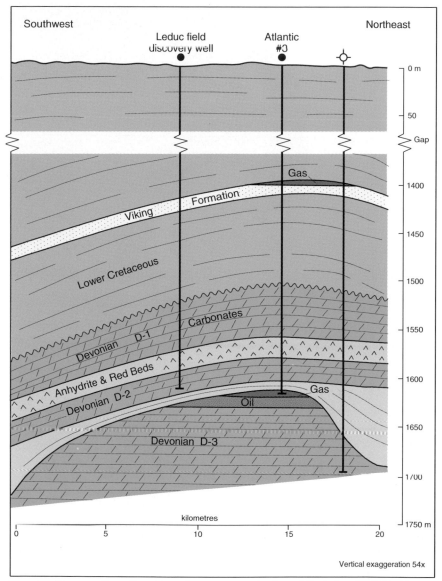

Figure 32. Diagrammatic southwest-to-northeast cross section through the Leduc oil field. Rock types and structure outline several oil and gas zones: Viking Formation, D-1 dolomite, D-2 dolomite, D-3 dolomite (modified from Aubrey Kerr).

by great detective work by Mike Hriskevich and John Rudolph of

Aquitaine, to complete the northern picture.

Figure 33. Imperial Leduc Number 1, February 13, 1947.

Provincial Archives of Alberta, No. P.2719

Viking oil was discovered downdip from the Viking - Kinsella gas field at Joseph Lake, Armena and Camrose (Joarcam) and at Joffre near Red Deer. The greatest discovery in Alberta was a dream of Ralph Rutherford of the Department of Geology. He had mapped in the foothills and observed a thick sandstone and conglomerate bed in the Colorado Shale, known as the Cardium Member. This sandstone did not occur in the section at Leduc. As wildcats were spudded west from the Leduc field searching for other Golden Spike fields, Rutherford would point to a new well location and say to me – watch this one! It was in 1954, two years after Rutherford's death that Arne Nielsen and Tony Mason of Mobil Oil encountered and tested the Cardium sandstone in a wildcat well along the Pembina River, and the Pembina oilfield was born. The Cardium sandstone had pinched out in a huge arc, trapping nearly 400 million cubic metres of light oil between Colorado shales of Cretaceous age.

The Leduc play was responsible for the development of the refinery row in Edmonton. Imperial started with an old refinery. This had been set up in the 1940s to refine Norman Wells oil transported to Whitehorse in the Yukon via the Alcan pipeline. This serviced army traffic along the Alcan Highway and the airline corridor to Alaska for a short time when the Japanese were invading the Aleutians and the future of Alaska and indeed North America appeared to be at stake. Other more modern refineries followed and Edmonton became the terminus for two important oil pipelines –

Ralph Leslie Rutherford (1894-1952)

Rutherford was born in Middleville, Ontario, and moved to Edmonton as a youth in 1907. He received his academic training at the University of Alberta, the Massachusetts Institute of Technology, and the University of Wisconsin before joining the staff of the University of Alberta in 1923.

In 1917, Rutherford worked as a field assistant under J.A. Allan and in 1920 joined the Scientific and Industrial Research Council of Alberta (now the Alberta Research Council) as a field geologist. Much of Rutherford's field research was centred on interpreting the structure and subsurface geology of the foothills belt and adjacent plains. This work not only led to a better understanding of Foothills coal deposits but also assisted in the subsequent exploration and development of petroleum resources in the region.

Ralph Rutherford was a close friend of many of Alberta's early oilmen, and in his conversations with them he loved to bring the academic viewpoint to the "game" of oil exploration. From the time of discovery of the Turner Valley field until his death, he kept a geological map of the Foothills and plotted the location of every well drilled in the area. Rutherford and his map were frequently consulted by students, colleagues and oilmen.

Interprovincial going east to Toronto, Trans Mountain going west to Vancouver. This was followed by the Alberta Gas Trunkline (Nova) and TransCanada PipeLines designed to carry surplus gas to eastern markets and Alberta Natural Gas and Pacific Gas Transmission carrying gas south to California. A host of product pipelines now tie the province into knots, and serve a burgeoning petrochemical industry.

The search for oil in Alberta is waning. Perhaps all the giant fields have been found. Increasingly the majors are going after the heavy oils with Suncor and Syncrude dipping into Peter's miraculous pond at Fort McMurray with other majors, and Imperial, BP Canada and Husky huffing and puffing at Cold Lake, Primrose and refinery upgrading of heavy oil at Lloydminster. Imperial is looking at Oslo (oh so slow), the other seven leases at Fort McMurray, the potential site of the next bituminous sand plant.

The natural gas story is far from finished. Exploring north and south from Turner Valley in the Rocky Mountain front, huge gas fields were discovered at Waterton, Savannah Creek, Jumping Pound, Stolberg and Ram River, mostly in Mississippian carbonates which also produce gas and condensate in the plains in pinchouts at Sundre and Edson. Caroline is the southernmost of the Leduc chain of reservoirs, with 30 billion m³ of hydrogen sulphide rich gas in reserve.

The search has extended into northeastern British Columbia with success at Fort St. John and Fort Nelson.

A last, but not least example. In the early forties, pre-Leduc, Charlie Stelck, newly graduated from the University of Alberta, sat on a well drilled by the Government of British Columbia, ostensibly on the crest of the Commotion Creek anticline in the Monkman Pass area west of Fort St. John. British Columbia was desperate for an oil or gas discovery of Turner Valley type. Charlie has always maintained that the well was mistakenly drilled on the east flank of the anticline and that it remained in vertically tilted Cretaceous quartzitic sandstones – the Bullhead Formation. He would see vertical bedding planes in the cores, telling him that the sandstones, originally laid down horizontally, had been folded into a vertical position. After 3 km of terribly difficult drilling the well was abandoned, still in the Bullhead Formation. Bull headed indeed!

Using modern 3D seismic information, BP Canada and Ocelot Resources have successfully interpreted the anticlinal structures in the Bull Moose area and have brought in eight successful wells drilled through the Cretaceous Bullhead Formation into limestone reservoirs of the Upper Triassic, rich in natural gas. This is an unusual gas, rich in methane, carbon dioxide (for carbonated beverages and as a prod to reluctant oil reservoirs) and hydrogen sulphide (for sulphuric acid). Each well defines 3 billion m³ of gas. There are one hundred well locations on the identified anticlines and the prediction is that the Sukunka - Bull Moose area will become Canada's largest gas reservoir, with recoverable reserves of 180 to 200 billion m³ of gas. This is almost as much gas as in the gas cap at Prudhoe Bay, for which a $5 billion pipeline heading for Alaska across Alberta, British Columbia and the Yukon was proposed. Perhaps it is fortunate that the prebuilt pipeline extends just to the Monkman Pass area, a stones throw from the newly discovered gas field. Edmonton, the oil centre of Canada, will be replaced by Fort St. John, Canada's natural gas centre!

The oil industry in Western Canada has had heady days. They may come again. But it is a sobering thought that the generous gift shed on the land of the Blue-eyed Arabs will never approach that of Arabia.

Salt of Life

Wylie N. Hamilton

The Edmonton region seems an unlikely place as a centre for chemical manufacturing because of its inland location and distance from high-density population areas and markets. However, chemical manufacturing is a strong industry in the region, made possible by the availability of three essential industrial mineral commodities: salt, sulphur and limestone. These commodities are the raw materials of the chemical industry and enter into the processes of nearly all chemical manufacturing. Another big factor is the abundance of natural gas, the fuel favoured by many industrial operations because it is relatively inexpensive, clean and convenient. Indeed, it is because of the availability of natural gas at low cost in the region that raw materials can be brought in from afar as a base for some industries.

The first industrial mineral for consideration is one that we see every day on our dinner table – *salt* (sodium chloride). However, few of us ever see the mineral in its natural geological state, which in the Edmonton region is more than 2 km beneath our feet. Salt deposits underlie a vast area of Alberta

(Figure 34), and if you are standing in southwest Edmonton, you are just at the western limit of the salt beds. The salt beds thicken significantly to the northeast, and at Fort Saskatchewan are

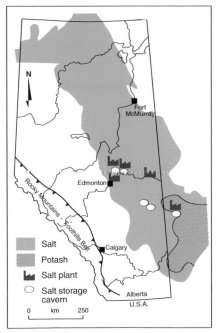

Figure 34. Extent of salt deposits in Alberta, ranging in depth from 220 m at Fort McMurray to 2000 m at Edmonton.

about 60 m thick. Farther northeast, toward Bruderheim, the salt beds are about 75 m thick and are closer to the surface updip at about 1750 m depth. Hence, most industrial operations that are based on raw salt are located in the northeast Edmonton - Fort Saskatchewan region. Now let's take a look at some of these operations.

At Fort Saskatchewan, Dow Chemical Canada Ltd. mines salt from beds deeper than 1,850 m for manufacturing chemicals such as chlorine and caustic soda (sodium hydroxide). The salt is produced by a brining operation, in which fresh water is pumped down a well drilled into the salt bed and circulated to dissolve the salt, which is brought to the surface in the form of a saturated salt brine. This brine is then treated and subjected to a process known as electrolysis, which separates the chemical components of the salt into caustic soda and chlorine gas.

Chlor-alkali manufacturing has been a growth industry for the Edmonton region, valued at around $100 million annually. The value of raw salt alone, consumed at the Dow plant, is about $12 million. However, the main market for these chemical products, the pulp and paper industry, is now looking at substitute chemicals for some parts of its operations, particularly the use of chlorine in its pulp-bleaching process. A chemical that is much more environmentally friendly than chlorine is the compound chlorine dioxide, also a product of salt although produced by a more indirect process. To make chlorine dioxide, you start with an intermediate chemical, sodium

chlorate, which is manufactured directly from salt brine, also by electrolysis. Sodium chlorate is subsequently converted at the pulp mill to chlorine dioxide, as required.

Growth in demand for sodium chlorate, because of its environmentally preferred status, has led to the building of two new plants in the Bruderheim area, by CanadianOxy Chemicals Group and Albchem Industries Ltd. These plants were recently completed at costs of $62 million and $45 million, respectively, and have a combined annual capacity of 105,000 tonnes of sodium chlorate. The value of these two new operations, at full production, could be about $50 million annually.

Another important use of the vast salt resource is for underground storage of petroleum products. The storage is provided in huge salt caverns created by washing out cavities in the salt beds. The products stored in these caverns can include natural gas, propane, butanes and pentanes, petrochemicals, and even crude oil; all can be stored safely and inexpensively in these facilities with only minimal surface installations required. Six such storage operations exist in the Fort Saskatchewan area, operated by Amoco Canada Ltd., Chevron Standard Ltd., Dow Chemical Canada Ltd., M-P Petroleum Ltd., Northwestern Utilities Ltd., and Procor Ltd. The value of these storage facilities to the region is difficult to determine, but the equivalent cost in surface tank storage is in the millions of dollars. The negligible surface impact and the safety aspect of this type of underground storage speaks strongly in favour of its increased use in the future, and provides an added dimension to a resource, or in this case to its predetermined "absence", that we never get to see.

Looking again at the Fort Saskatchewan area, we observe another important Alberta resource being put to use. *Sulphur* is the province's most valuable industrial mineral product after oil and gas. Most of the sulphur production comes as a byproduct of natural sour gas processing throughout the western part of the Province (Figure 35). The availability of low-cost sulphur and natural gas supplies has led to the rise of Alberta's fertilizer industry, which is concentrated in the Edmonton region. There are two major fertilizer plants, one operated by Sherritt Gordon Ltd. at Fort Saskatchewan and the other by Esso Resources Ltd. at Redwater. Along with sulphur, the principal raw materials used at these plants are ammonia, produced on site by reacting air and steam with natural gas, and phosphate rock, which is hauled by boat and rail from Florida. Transporting bulky low-unit value materials such as phosphate rock from distant places is not normally economically viable, but is made possible in this case through a back-haul arrangement with Saskatchewan potash. The combined value of fertilizer production at these two plants is about $300 million annually, and therefore is a major contributor to the economy of the region.

Sherritt Gordon's industrial complex at Fort Saskatchewan also includes a

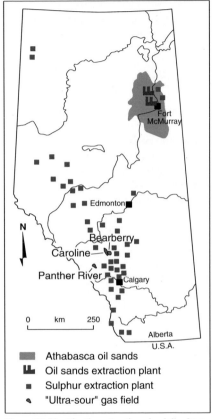

Figure 35. Plant for the extraction of sulphur from sour gas.

nickel-refining plant. The nickel concentrate feed was initially obtained from mines in Manitoba, but substantial foreign supplies are now being used. One of the industrial chemicals used in the refining process is anhydrous ammonia, a leaching agent for the recovery of metals. Ammonia is produced on site, but the capacity was greater than that initially required by the metals plant. This led the company to begin fertilizer manufacture, and demonstrates the adaptability of an industry in maximizing the use of resources at hand.

Sherritt Gordon's production of extremely high purity metallic nickel has gained the company a position as one of the world's major centres of nickel coin production, and a significant proportion of the western world's coinage is produced here. The extensive metallurgical research that went into design and production of Canada's "Loonie" was conducted at the company's Fort Saskatchewan plant.

The third primary raw material for chemicals manufacturing is *limestone*. In the Edmonton region the main use of limestone is not in the manufacture of chemicals, but for making cement. Cement is one essential component (along with aggregate) of concrete, a principal construction material. In northwest Edmonton, the plant owned by Inland Cement Ltd. is one of the major cement production facilities in Western Canada. Another cement plant in northeast Edmonton, operated by Lafarge Canada Inc., does not manufacture cement, but is a grinding facility for cement clinker produced in Exshaw, Alberta. The Inland Cement plant obtains its limestone from Cadomin, in the Alberta Foothills southwest of Edson. This is the nearest source of limestone for Edmonton and the rock is hauled by rail from Cadomin, a distance of 280 km. The plant receives an 80-car shipment once a week, and at full capacity consumes about 900,000 tonnes of limestone per

year. The exact value of cement production in the Edmonton region is not currently made public; however, recent figures for total production from the Edmonton and Exshaw plants have ranged from $100 million to $126 million.

Other industrial mineral operations in the region, although not as highly valued, are still important to the local economy. One of these is a *gypsum* wallboard plant in northeast Edmonton owned by Domtar Construction Materials Ltd. This is the source for much of the drywall that goes into homes and offices in Edmonton and throughout northern Alberta. Gypsum raw material for this plant comes from the Windermere Valley of southeastern British Columbia, a haul distance of 700 km. This is a very long haul for gypsum and a high-cost item for the plant, but there are no closer sources. Alberta has gypsum deposits but no gypsum production and must rely on outside sources for all its requirements, which for the Domtar plant can be up to 75,000 tonnes per year at full capacity. The value of wallboard production at this plant is estimated at about $6 million annually.

Gypsum finds other uses. It is an important ingredient in cement making, where it is blended into the final product to act as a setting retardant. The Inland Cement and Lafarge Canada plants together consume about 30,000 tonnes annually in their product output. Most of this gypsum also comes from southeastern British Columbia.

The last commodity that is worthy of mention is *peat moss*. In the eyes of some, peat moss is not a mineral but is a plant (Sphagnum). Nevertheless, it is extracted like a mineral, and the Edmonton region is blessed with an abundance of this resource. Its potential importance as an agent in environmental protection (for example, this absorbent material is used to soak up spills of oil or toxic wastes) makes it a resource to watch in the future. The region has a long history of production, both of processed and unprocessed material, mainly for horticultural use. Currently, only one small processing plant operates in northwest Edmonton, for drying, shredding, baling and bagging peat. The value of peat moss production in the region is unknown, but is probably less than one-tenth the total for Alberta, which is $15 million annually. Most of Alberta's production comes from west of Edmonton, near Lake Wabamun.

4

LEARNING THE GROUND RULES

Engineering Geology

David Cruden and Stanley Thomson

■ Introduction

The geological knowledge we need to construct a large, technologically safe and modern city is acquired gradually by experience with natural materials and processes at sites around the city. These sites are rarely chosen for engineering reasons. The North Saskatchewan River brought the fur trade to Edmonton House, the head of practical navigation on the river, and the river valley dominated the growing settlement. Two experiences, the Grierson Hill landslide and the 1915 flood, have kept most of us at a respectful distance from the river; these natural hazards are described in the first section of this chapter.

The natural materials underlying the City form part of the city's infrastructure; they react to the loads that our buildings and utilities impose on them. Sometimes these reactions are strong enough to require changes in design or construction. These constraints are discussed in the two sections "Going Underground" and "Foundations".

The City's population generates waste materials which we now realize cannot carelessly be thrown away. Their treatment is discussed in the section entitled "To Inter is Human."

■ Distance Lends Enchantment

James MacGregor's *History of Edmonton* contains a year-by-year list of Historical Highlights. Nothing is recorded for 1901, but it was a traumatic year for the residents of Cliffe Street which ran westward from 95th Street (then Kirkness Street), south of what is now 101st Avenue. Bob Edwards, then illuminating *The Alberta Sun* in Strathcona, had cast Edmontonians as "cliff-dwellers" before he headed south to open the eyes of Calgarians. Cliffe Street headed over the cliffs, down to the flats of Rossdale where the still incomplete Low Level Bridge, battered by the floods of 1899 and 1900, waited to bring the Edmonton, Yukon and Pacific Railroad across the North Saskatchewan River.

The Edmonton Bulletin (September 27, 1901) reported, *"The wet weather of the last two seasons has brought to a crisis the impending land slides along the hill face in the eastern end of town. The situation has now become one of grave importance to property holders along the stretch affected, a distance of some 500 yards. ... Along the hill front the earth is splitting and sinking, the face of the hill sliding downward. These cracks run in different places, but always parallel to the river and about twenty feet back from the hill brow. Fortunately,* buildings along this stretch are not numerous and those that are there are of a nature to be readily moved, with one or two exceptions (Figure 36). Several property holders along this stretch are now taking precautions to guard against going over the hill by moving their buildings (Figure 37) ... The slides have made material alterations in the topography of the locality. The flat around Humberstone's coal mine has not escaped. Lying as it does just below the high bank where all the big slides have occurred the contortions of the country have affected it to the extent of putting all the houses out of plumb and temporarily interfering with the mining of coal at Humberstone's mine. His house is also cracking. An odd feature of the slides is that of all the earth that has changed places it is impossible to see where any of it has gone. ... The cracking and sliding still continues. Much difference of opinion exists as to the cause. Three causes are assigned: The action of the rains, undermining by the river, and undermining by coal shafts. It is claimed that the damage to the property in front of the Columbia was due in the first place to the explosion of a great deal of dynamite there on the last 4th of July. These explosions opened cracks in the earth in which the water soaked and did the rest. These slides are confined to the east end of town and to a single row of lots abutting on the high bank of the valley. They are east of the business and principal residential portions of the town which are not affected, even along the brow of the hill. The slides are confined to the part under which coal mining has been principally carried on."

The year 1901 was certainly wet; July 1901 is still the wettest month Edmonton has experienced. The 280

Figure 36. View looking northwest along the north bank of the North Saskatchewan River valley showing the eastern flank of the active Grierson Hill landslide in the fall of 1901.

Provincial Archives of Alberta, Ernest Brown Collection B9-82

Figure 37. Kitchen(?) extension split from the main house by landslide scarp, south of Mr. Graham's house?

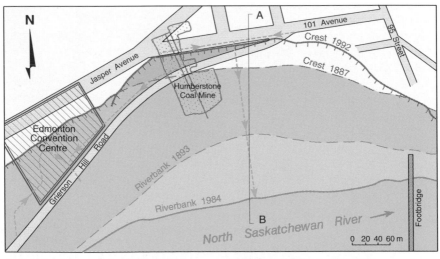

Subsurface drainage   Landslide escarpment

Figure 38. A plan view of Grierson Hill showing the landslide area and recent remedial works.

mm of rain recorded is more than three times the average precipitation for July, usually the wettest month of the year here. It followed the wettest year in Edmonton's history. Nearly 750 mm of precipitation fell in 1900, almost 60 percent above average. The Bulletin reported the slides began on July 21, after a severe hailstorm on July 18 produced 50 mm of moisture in an hour or so.

River erosion was also extreme; old maps show 15 m of bank removed from the 1887 bank to leave the 1893 bank shown in Figure 38. Then in 1897, the construction of the piers for the Low Level Bridge began to alter river flow downstream, perhaps promoting scour. In 1899 and 1900, the summer floods reached levels which have since only been exceeded by the 1915 flood. Two and a half metres had to be added to the height of the bridge piers.

Humberstone's miners removed 9,000 tonnes of coal from the river bank. Smaller mines had also contributed to the cracking and subsidence of the Cretaceous Edmonton Group rocks and the overlying sands, till and lake clays (Figure 39). One cause the Bulletin missed; it lay within the coal seams. James Hector, the Palliser Expedition geologist had described the seams 40 years earlier noting *"In the middle of the 6-foot seam, there occurs a layer 5 to 8 inches thick of magnesium steutitic clay which works up into a lather like soap and is used by the women at the Fort for washing blankets"*. Grierson Hill then slid slowly riverward on these soapy clay layers which were later shown to be mostly the clay mineral, *montmorillonite*, now used as an active component of drilling

muds for the oil industry and clay liners for landfills.

Seven buildings and the Humberstone coal mine were damaged by the 1901 movements. Sliding continued, and by 1915 nine more buildings had been affected. The sunken block at the head of the slide mysteriously attracted garbage and the weight of this fill on the head of the slide drove the toe farther downslope. The protected river bank is now more than 100 m south of its turn-of-the century natural position.

Fill at the toe of the slope stabilized it sufficiently for a steep haul road to be developed to the Gallagher landfill. Photographs taken in 1931 show that above the dump the steep scarp of the landslide still edged Jasper Avenue (Figure 40). In 1949, City Council decided to pave Grierson Hill Road but, first, more fill was needed to widen the road and reduce the slope of its eastern end. The fill reactivated the slide and the Dean of Engineering at the University of Alberta, Dr. R.M. Hardy, was consulted. He recommended drainage. Wells were installed and pumped and as they were successful in slowing movements, a gravity drainage tunnel was driven in 1957; it drained Humberstone's mine and allowed the completion of the road embankment in 1961. The road was paved in 1963, but small movements continue to dislocate it. In 1969, deeper exploration rediscovered Hector's soapy clays and new computer techniques of slope stability analysis showed that they underlaid the persistent southward downslope journey of Grierson Hill.

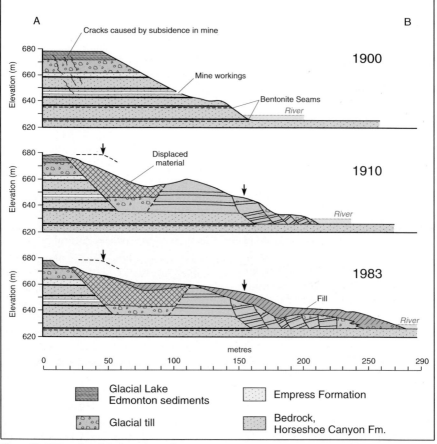

Figure 39. This series of three north-south sections through the Grierson Hill landslide shows the progressive change from 1900, 1910 to 1983 along the line A - B in Figure 38. Cretaceous bedrock underlies Empress Formation, till and glacial lake sediments.

Grading and landscaping of Grierson Hill in 1978 for the Capital City Park set the scene for the construction of the City's Convention Centre on the western flank of the 1901 slide. Before the weight of the Centre loaded the slope, a deep excavation removed more than the Centre's weight in ground. The back of the excavation was supported by a continuous wall of concrete piles installed before any

digging steepened the slope. As the piles were gradually exposed by the deepening excavation they were anchored to the slope by long steel cables cemented into holes drilled through the piles and back under Jasper Avenue (Figure 26). With experience, careful observation of how the ground reacted, and this sophisticated technology, the City has been able to reclaim some of the ground lost ninety years ago. The view of the river which attracted the early cliff dwellers can now be enjoyed from the comfort and safety of the Edmonton Convention Centre terraces.

Figure 40. Grierson Hill, May 8, 1931.

Upper: looking west along the north bank of the North Saskatchewan River valley toward the Low Level Bridge, Legislature and the Hotel Macdonald. The Gallagher landfill site is in the foreground.

Lower: looking east from the furniture warehouse (see upper photograph) immediately east of the Hotel Macdonald.

As it is now more distant, perhaps it is more enchanting.

A distant and safe view of a smaller landslide, on the south bank of the North Saskatchewan River below Lavigne (Skunk Hollow), is described in Chapter 5 (Site 5). The Rossdale Power Plant gives access to a dramatic sweep of the river which has continually steepened the bank on the outside of the curve.

■ Dampers

Large floods on the North Saskatchewan River and its tributaries at Edmonton are caused primarily by torrential rainfall rather than snow melt. Snowmelt however creates the saturated ground conditions which cause large runoffs. This period of saturation extends yearly from April to June. Thus, a large rainstorm during the spring or early summer could trigger substantial flows. The 1972 flood, for instance, was caused by a heavy rainstorm that moved northwestward into Alberta along the Foothills of the Rockies in late June. The weather system mixed warm moist air with cold Arctic air directing flow toward the mountains. The air was forced to rise by the mountain front; as it rose it cooled, and as it cooled it became saturated and heavy rainfall resulted from what is known as upslope conditions. The earliest annual flood peak occurred on April 12, 1943, the latest on September 4, 1926. On average the flood peak occurs on June 29th.

Alberta Environment has mapped out the flood plains of the North Saskatchewan River through Edmonton for 50-, 75- and 100-year floods. They extend over much of the low level terraces. The flood of June 28 - 29, 1915, described next, approximated the 100-year flood. Comparable flows in 1899 and 1900 predate continuous records of the flow of the North Saskatchewan River; accurate statistics began in 1911. The 100-year flood has a one-in-a-hundred chance of occurring each year. If you live on the flood plain all your life, you are more likely to see this flood than not.

Since the 1915 flood, the city has been protected by two dams, the Bighorn and the Brazeau. Alberta Environment's report noted that *"under ideal conditions, the maximum-possible, combined effect of the two dams would be a reduction of approximately 1.2 m (4 ft) in river stage in Edmonton ... Since many of the factors affecting flood peak reduction are nebulous and difficult to quantify ... Any effect that the Bighorn and Brazeau Dams do have should be considered as a small safety factor incorporated into the derived water surface elevations."*

A contemporary account of the 1915 flood reported *"The greatest amount of damage done was at Edmonton where the direct losses were estimated at from one half to three quarters of a million dollars ... due to the inundating of the lower parts of the town known as Fraser, Ross and Mill Creek and Gallagher Flats, the washing away of the Edmonton Lumber Company's mill and the destruction of booms belonging to the Edmonton Lumber Company and the Walter's sawmills (Figure 41). Many homes were destroyed and the damages to hundreds of others and their contents were very great. It is estimated that 800 families*

City of Edmonton Archives E-10-892

Figure 41. View looking east from the south end of the High Level Bridge. Overlooking Walter's Sawmill with the North Saskatchewan River at flood stage and the flood plain under water, June 1915.

were rendered homeless by the flood. The loss of life was fortunately very light, the only casualty being an infant which was dropped by its mother from a floating sidewalk into the flooded street ... There was a depth of 10 feet of water at some points on the flats. The electric light and water pumping plants were out of commission for some hours owing to the flooding of their boiler fires and this caused considerable inconvenience to a number of businesses and residents in the higher parts of the city ... The Low Level Bridge was in danger owing to debris such as buildings, sidewalks, logs and roots collecting on the piers and bridge stringers, but this structure was saved by cleaning this debris away and by placing a loaded train on the bridge (Figure 42)".

The losses, none of which would have been insured, place this flood among Edmonton's most expensive natural disasters. Even today, homeowners should note that their insurance

policies exclude losses from *"certain events ... because of their unmanageable nature"* as one policy describes *"natural disasters of water (i.e. floods) or earth movement."* Policies also exclude losses from *"a building's own movement as it settles"*, something to keep in mind while reading the next sections.

■ Going Underground

We have seen that most of the early settlers had little trouble moving their houses out of the way of the Grierson Hill slide. The structures were comparatively light and were not connected to fixed underground utilities. As the City grew, more services were provided. At the end of 1905, Edmonton had 9 km of sewers and more than 20 km of water mains

City of Edmonton Archives EA-160-1399

Figure 42. Low Level Bridge stabilized by an Edmonton, Yukon and Pacific Railroad train unit during the June, 1915 flood. Hotel Macdonald in background.

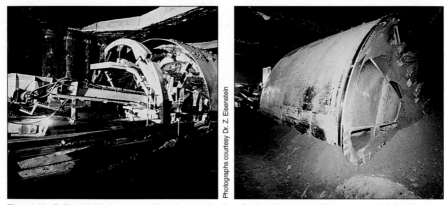

Photographs courtesy Dr. Z. Eisenstein

Figure 43. Fully-shielded mole passing through the Bay Station, downtown Edmonton, which had been excavated to the spring line in the tunnel.

which served perhaps a fifth of the City's population. Edmonton was growing underground. The increasing sophistication of the City required more detailed knowledge of the behaviour of the ground on which the City was being built. Subsurface information is crucial in the planning of tunnels and

in the design of the foundations of the larger buildings.

There are now several hundred kilometres of tunnels under the City of Edmonton, ranging from 1.5 m to 6 m in diameter. Tunnelling in Edmonton now employs either a tunnelling machine, called a mole (Figure 43), or a

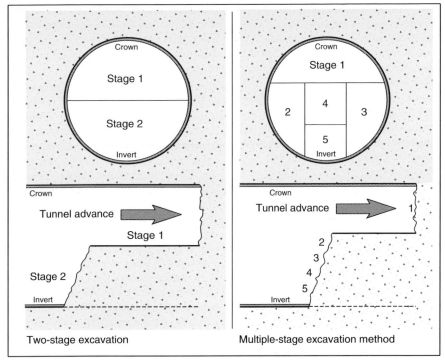

Two-stage excavation

Multiple-stage excavation method

Figure 44. Tunnel excavation by two Sequential Excavation Methods.

technique that excavates parts of the tunnel face in a set order, the Sequential Excavation Method. The mole is a steel tube containing the motor and controls of a rotating cutting head at the front of the tube and a series of jacks at the rear. The wheel-shaped cutting head has teeth mounted on a set of spokes and pie-shaped gates between the spokes that may be opened or closed to control the amount of material being excavated. This spoil is removed from behind the gates by a belt system that conveys it to hopper cars. As the mole advances, a temporary lining, consisting of steel ribs and wood lagging, stabilizes the tunnel until a final concrete lining is constructed.

The Sequential Excavation Method (SEM) works because a small tunnel is more stable than a large tunnel. Figure 44 shows the upper part of the tunnel face, the crown, advanced a short distance and stabilized by shotcrete, sprayed-on concrete. A section of the lower part is then excavated and stabilized. The advance of parts of the tunnel face continues until the full tunnel diameter has been excavated. The sequence is then repeated to advance the tunnel again. The number of sections of the face excavated sequentially depends on the size and shape of the tunnel and the type of ground being excavated.

In both tunnelling methods, the excavated spoil is removed from the face to the tunnel portal where it is loaded onto trucks for disposal. Spoil from a downtown tunnel was used to stabilize a slope in the Rat Creek Ravine, reducing it from 26° to a more stable slope of 14° that could be landscaped. The shorter haul to the landslide rather than to a disposal area reduced the cost of stabilizing the landslide.

Except where the Light Rail Transit System (LRT) goes underground at the tunnel portals, the tunnels are below the clayey Glacial Lake Edmonton sediments, in the till, in the Empress Formation, or in Cretaceous bedrock.

The till is good material for tunnelling because it will stand up until the temporary lining for the tunnel can be installed. Problems occur, however, when boulders in the till are too big to pass through the gates of the cutting wheel of the mole. These boulders have to be broken up with jackhammers to pass through the gates of the mole, a time-consuming chore in the very confined space right behind the cutting head.

The till also contains water-filled sand pockets up to one metre in diameter and half a metre thick. If the mole cuts into a sand pocket in the crown of the tunnel, the sand runs out and leaves a hole immediately above the tunnel lining. On rare occasions, the run through this hole extends to the ground surface and can create a hazardous depression. In any case, the void must be filled to prevent its upward growth. Filling the voids requires holes through the tunnel liner for injecting the grout,

usually a cement-sand mixture. The till also has natural vertical fractures, and fracture-bounded blocks have dropped out of the tunnel roof, leaving voids to be grouted.

Tunnelling through a sand mass is very difficult because the sand runs readily. In Edmonton, large sand masses infill the buried preglacial channels and form their terraces. These deposits, called the Empress Formation, are usually clean and medium- to fine-grained. Another sand source is glacial outwash which is fine-grained and contains some silt sizes. These sand units are difficult to inject with a grout that will keep the sand in place and prevent it flowing into the tunnel. Fortunately, most of the tunnels are above the water table. While dry sand runs readily, sand below the water table flows even more quickly into any void because of the groundwater pressure. Tunnelling through sand requires a special tunneling machine termed a hydroshield. In this equipment, drilling mud between the cutting head and a water-tight bulkhead holds the sand in place as the tunnelling machine advances. The excavated sand, suspended in the mud, is pumped from the face through screens that extract the sand. On one occasion, the sand being tunnelled contained boulders up to 45 cm in diameter. These jammed the pumping system circulating the mud and temporarily stopped the tunnel advance. Manual clearing of the boulders added to the cost . The boulders in the sand were not indicated by the exploratory drill holes, though in hindsight, their occurrence is readily explained as a lag deposit from the erosion of the till and subsequently incorporated into the sand.

The major, sandfilled preglacial buried valleys in Edmonton are now mapped (Figure 16) but the shallower tributary valleys are not as well known. In tunneling storm sewers, the mole has intercepted or passed close to the bottoms of these tributary valleys. Sudden flows of sand halt progress until the sand can be stabilized. If tunnelling were to continue, the sand would keep flowing into the tunnel and result in a large and, perhaps, deep depression at the ground surface. The sand may be stabilized by freezing as a cold brine is circulated through pipes installed into the sand mass from the tunnel.

Tunnelling through the Cretaceous bedrock is usually relatively straightforward, although the top part of the bedrock may be weathered and therefore much softer than the fresh rock. This factor is of importance when the Sequential Excavation Method is used to advance the tunnel rather than a mole. In those areas where sand rests on the bedrock, particular care must be taken where the crown of the tunnel is close to the upper surface of the bedrock in the softer weathered zone. If not adequately supported, the soft bedrock may sag downward and crack, allowing the sand to cascade into the tunnel. This material loss from above the tunnel can show as a depression at the ground surface. The bedrock is also jointed and because the bedrock surface is commonly below the water table, these joints may channel water under a hydraulic head into the tunnel.

Groundwater within the city usually does not present problems in tunnelling because the water table is deep and the till and bedrock are relatively impervious. On the lower terraces of the river, however, the water table is close to the ground surface. Just upstream of the LRT bridge on the south side of the river is the underground water intake and plant for the air conditioning system at the University of Alberta. This deep structure is, of course, waterproofed and had to be anchored to the underlying bedrock to prevent it from being floated upward out of the ground by North Saskatchewan River water pressures acting on it.

Where possible, it is more economical to avoid a problem rather than to engineer a solution. In one instance, where the LRT entered the northeast part of the University campus, boreholes along the proposed tunnel alignment revealed a buried sand mass. Rather than tunnelling through the sand, further exploratory boreholes to the west found a new route that avoided the sand mass, and possibly unstable ground.

The initial design of the Grandin LRT station required the removal of elm trees along the boulevard. These beautiful mature trees were saved by a modified design that placed the tangent pile wall at a slant to pass under the roots of the trees. Computer simulations of the structure augmented the design, and the wall and station were successfully completed.

Where a tunnel passes underneath a building, the crown of the tunnel is reinforced, particularly if the tunnel is only a few metres below the building foundation. The building is monitored to ensure the extra tunnel support is adequate. Precise levelling surveys determine the elevation of points established on the building. Elevations are checked regularly as the advancing tunnel face nears the building and continuing until the tunnel face is well past it. Most buildings can settle 15 to 20 mm without causing significant damage or distress. As an illustration, the LRT tunnel passed under HUB Mall at the University of Alberta within about 3 m of the base of the piles that form the foundations. The tunnel was being advanced by SEM and, under HUB, the crown was additionally reinforced. Elevations of points on both sides and inside HUB were surveyed as the tunnel advanced, and the settlement of the structure was less than the allowable 15 mm (Figure 45).

■ Foundations

For light structures such as houses and one- and two-storey buildings, the foundations or footings are strips of concrete on which the walls are placed, or are squares of concrete for interior columns. Within the City, these foundations are located about 2 m deep into the glacial lake clay. This sediment contains the clay mineral, montmorillonite, which has a strong affinity for water, swelling as water is adsorbed and shrinking as drying occurs. The pressure exerted by this swelling clay is high enough to heave light structures and basement floor slabs. Unsightly cracking of the structure occurs and in some cases

expensive remedial measures are required. In dry weather, the clay shrinks away from basement walls, leaving a gap that is quickly filled with water from rain or lawn watering. This water runs down to the footing level and heaving results. Maintaining the natural water content of the clay avoids problems from alternating swelling and shrinking. To achieve a stable condition (Figure 46), grade the surface of the ground at the outer walls of the structure to slope away from the building, discharge water from eavestroughs well away from the building (but not onto adjacent property), install a perimeter drain or weeping tile at footing level and avoid excessive lawn watering. These procedures keep water away from the clay soil adjacent to the structural foundations. The surface slope away from the building, and the eavestrough and perimeter drains all require careful maintenance as ground conditions and drainage systems can change with time.

In the south and west of the City, the Glacial Lake Edmonton clay at surface is replaced by a silt that is prone to heaving when frost penetrates the ground and encounters water which freezes. This frozen water draws additional water to the frost front and an ice lens grows, heaving the ground surface. The frost may penetrate deeper and another ice lens may form. In the spring, thawing takes place from the ground surface downward and, as the ice lens melts, water accumulates softening the surrounding soil. Traffic quickly creates a pothole, a mudfilled hazard to travel. The completion of thawing allows the water to drain away

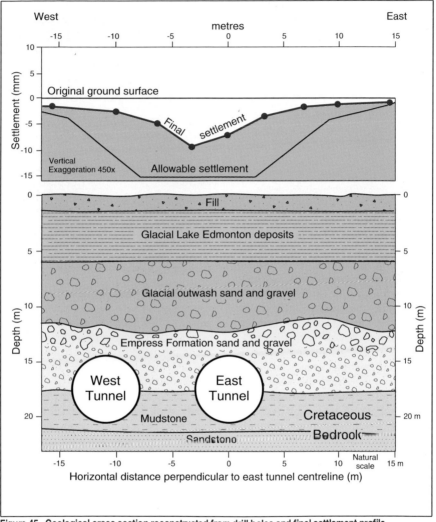

Figure 45. Geological cross section reconstructed from drill holes and final settlement profile perpendicular to the two Light Rail Transit (LRT) tunnels after construction at 110 Street and 97 Avenue. The east tunnel is northbound and the west tunnel is southbound. Note difference of vertical scales and exaggerations in the two parts of this figure.

and the mudhole soon dries to become a dust-filled hole. In paved areas, the pavement is broken up and the driving hazard multiplies. Repairs are costly.

The City is experimenting with styrofoam-insulated road pavements to reduce frost penetration.

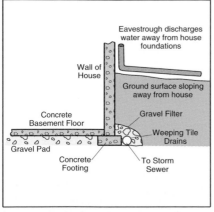

Figure 46. Typical house foundation details.

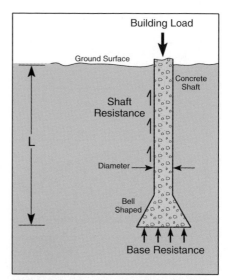

Figure 47. Cast-in-place concrete pile; the shaft diameter commonly ranges from 0.3 to 0.9 m and its length (L) ranges from 6 m to 20 m.

Although cast-in-place concrete piles are more common, a few large structures in Edmonton have been founded on spread footings, thick slabs of reinforced concrete that transmit the building loads to the underlying ground. However, these footings must be placed below the lake clays on the more competent underlying till, sand or bedrock. All of these three materials have a high bearing capacity and are strong enough to carry the weight of the building. Settlement, downward movement due to the weight of the structure, is normally within acceptable limits on these deposits.

The common cast-in-place, bell-shaped pile (Figure 47) consists of a bored hole with an enlarged base backfilled with concrete. The diameters of the shaft and base are designed to support the load imposed by the structure. Though a pile is straightforward to construct, care should be taken that the bottom of the pile is clean and any material that has fallen off the sides of the hole during boring is removed. Because sand will run readily into the borehole, the shaft is cased through any sand bed.

Cast-in-place piles placed in a row touching one another are termed tangent piles. They can form a retaining wall for deep excavations. This is the technique used in the construction of the LRT stations and at the Edmonton Convention Centre. Because the ground exerts a considerable pressure on the wall, the piles are reinforced with steel bars. As excavation proceeds, the concrete slab floors within a station act as struts between opposite rows of the tangent piles to take part of the load imposed on the pilewall by the ground and ensure the safety and integrity of the structure.

Even though the strata are able to carry large buildings, some foundation difficulties remain. Although the till is basically a strong material, it contains local narrow soft sandy zones. These zones are interpreted as infilled meltwater channels formed by the melting glaciers that deposited the till.

If a large building is partly founded on a soft zone and the rest on competent till, the soft zone part will settle more than the part on the strong till. This differential settlement causes severe stress in the framework of the building. In one instance downtown, the foundations had to be placed below the till onto the underlying dense sand, thereby increasing the foundation cost.

The turn-of-the-century coal mines have caused problems beyond Grierson Hill. The cast-in-place piles need to be placed in casings where passing through old mine workings into the underlying, undisturbed bedrock, the extra length and casing of the piles representing extra costs.

Research continues on construction methods within the City, studying the behaviour of the ground under various loading conditions and testing the validity of new design techniques and theories. This research enhances the capability of the engineer to create a more efficient design, while maintaining the safety and integrity of the structure. Collaboration between the project owner, the design and consulting engineers and the contractors is extremely valuable. One research project improved estimates of the settlement of large buildings in Edmonton. The Geotechnical Group in the Department of Civil Engineering at the University of Alberta evolved a technique that provides more precise and reliable estimates of settlement. Powerful computing codes have improved design capability but require validation by case histories, actual observed field data, before they can be used in practical design; the ground rules!

Solid Waste Management

Laurence D. Andriashek

■ To Inter is Human

Solid and liquid wastes must be handled in every human settlement, ranging from small farms to large cities like Edmonton. The natural environment has the ability to accept human wastes without long-term impact or stress, if quantities and concentrations are at low levels. However, as populations grow, the increased generation of waste places further demands on the natural systems to try and cope with the waste.

There is a general lack of knowledge of how presently designed modern landfills operate. Landfills conjure up images of huge piles of rotting debris, with flocks of seagulls ripping open plastic bags, of smoldering garbage, the air thick with flies, not to mention bad smells from the smoking refuse. However, engineered landfills today are very much different in their design and operation. To appreciate how far waste management has evolved, it is useful to compare the historical landfills of the Edmonton area with current landfill sites, in term of their criteria and construction designs.

The management of solid waste, or garbage, was the responsibility of the individual home owner in the early days of Edmonton. During the early 1900s, prior to the existence of an urban sanitary sewage system or garbage collection program, the backyards of many homes in Edmonton had outdoor toilets (outhouses) to contain human waste and burn-barrels to reduce solid waste. Although not an accepted practice, non-flammable items such as old car bodies, commonly found their way down the river banks or into a local ravine. From the early 1900s to the mid-1950s, an urban collection system gathered the City's waste for incineration at the site presently occupied by the Muttart Conservatory. Ash from the incinerator was disposed of in nearby abandoned gravel pits, and non-combustibles such as cans and other metal items were stockpiled nearby. These stockpiles were eventually covered with earth to form the core of Connors ski hill. The increasing amount of waste, combined with a general perception that the air was being polluted, led to the incineration process being abandoned in favour of the burial of solid waste at landfill sites.

Most early landfills in the Edmonton area were located in pre-existing depressions, either natural landscape features such as river banks and ravines, or man-made excavations such as sand and gravel, or borrow pits. From a pragmatic point-of-view, this approach makes sense. It is less expensive to fill an existing hole than to excavate a new one. The filling of old pits, excavations and low-lying areas with waste also allows a scarred, torn landscape, to be reclaimed and put into productive use.

The first large-scale waste disposal sites in Edmonton took advantage of abandoned gravel pits or river cuts along the North Saskatchewan River. An example is the Beverly landfill site, located on the north bank of the North Saskatchewan River, in the Rundle Heights district (Figure 48). The undulating to gently rolling fairways of the Rundle Heights Golf Course are founded on a thick mound of garbage. From the mid-1950s to the early 1970s, as much as 25 m of solid waste were deposited at the Beverly site. In addition to accepting industrial waste, the Beverly site was also the disposal site for old car bodies. In places, as much as 10 m of compressed cars

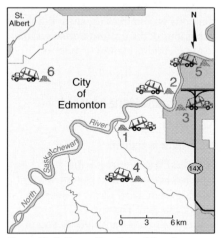

Figure 48. Active and inactive solid waste disposal sites in the Edmonton municipal area.
(1) Gallagher Site (Incinerator ash disposal) 1900 to 1950
(2) Beverly Site (1950 to 1975)
(3) Frontier Site (1970 to 1975)
(4) 75th Street (Millwoods) Site (1955 to 1975)
(5) Clover Bar Site (1975 to present)
(6) 170th Street (Yellowhead) Site (1980 to present)

underlie the landfill. The flattened car bodies were stacked by a bulldozer, forming a steep wall of crushed steel. When a fire started at the base of the wall of steel, plastics and other fabric from the car interiors fuelled the flames, creating an inferno that lasted for more than a week. The heat was so intense that the steel melted, forming a puddle of liquid metal. The metal solidified into an impermeable layer at the bottom of the stack.

During the time that the Beverly landfill site was active, a new landfill site was being prepared to accept waste, on the south side of the North Saskatchewan River. The 75th Street landfill site is located in Millwoods, south of Whitemud Drive and east of 75th Street. This landfill came into operation in the mid-1950s. Unlike the Beverly site, which was located on gravels next to the river, the 75th Street site was engineered on naturally clayey and impermeable soils. Draglines cut a series of east-west trenches into which alternating layers of solid waste and clayey soil were placed to a thickness greater than 12 m. This landfill ceased operation about 1975, and was then reclaimed to become a park and the Millwoods Golf Course.

Even though heavy equipment compacted the waste, uneven settlement has occurred at both the Beverly and 75th Street landfills. However, this is not necessarily undesirable. The rolling to hummocky topography has added more character to the originally levelled surface and created a more diverse terrain for these golf courses.

From the mid-1970s to the early 1990s, Edmonton has disposed of its solid waste at two major sites, the Clover Bar landfill in northeast Edmonton, and the 170th Street site north of the Yellowhead Trail in northwest Edmonton. The Clover Bar landfill is situated on a lower terrace of the North Saskatchewan River. Waste was placed in existing gravel pits in the terrace, but with time the height of the landfill rose above that of the natural terrace. Because the Clover Bar site is situated on permeable granular material and is adjacent to the river, steps have been taken to ensure that contaminated water, or leachate, does not leave the landfill. An impermeable liner was built at the base of the landfill, constructed from clayey material such as the clay tills or glaciolacustrine deposits that mantle the Edmonton area. About one metre of clayey material was placed over the entire floor and walls of the landfill. This clay-rich soil was then compacted with heavy equipment to ensure that all large voids were collapsed to prevent leachates flowing through the clayey liner and entering the river.

The other major Edmonton landfill currently in use is the 170th Street site, located directly north of Inland Cement on the Yellowhead Trail. Here, waste is being placed in abandoned pits which had supplied clay for the production of cement. Both the 170th Street and Clover Bar landfills are nearing the end of their useful lifespans, after more than 17 years of operation.

■ How Do Landfills Operate?

Industrial landfills must meet a number of rigourous conditions to ensure that they are environmentally acceptable. Industrial landfills receive both liquid and solid wastes, but not hazardous wastes such as radioactive materials or extremely toxic chemicals such as gasoline, organic solvents or medical wastes. In addition, they must meet strict engineering requirements. Two protective liners are used to contain leachate and other liquids in the landfill. At least one of the liners must be synthetic plastic and there must be a system for detecting leaks between the two liners. It must also be possible to collect and remove leachate or other liquids from the landfill and to prevent surface water from flowing onto or off the site. Explosive or toxic gases produced by decomposing buried wastes must also be removed. As a further safeguard, a monitoring system of observation wells is installed along the perimeter of the site to detect any change in the quality of groundwater.

Figure 49 is a cartoon depiction of how most modern landfills are designed and operated. Note that waste is disposed in a series of carefully engineered containment units (comprising lifts and cells) that are operated independently, each having its own lining and leachate collection systems. The lining system consists of two protective barriers, one is a flexible synthetic membrane, and the other is constructed from natural clay materials. The daily operation requires waste to be covered by compacted clay

to minimize exposure or communication with the environment. This procedure reduces bird and insect activity, and minimizes the exit of odours and wind-blown material from the site.

With time, leachate can accumulate at the base of the landfill, increasing the possibility that fluid pollutants can migrate from the site to contaminate the local groundwater. Leachate includes liquids such as surface water that has percolated through solid waste, and liquids introduced in association with the solid waste, such as decomposing organic materials. The characteristic features of a leachate are that it has a high organic content and has dissolved, suspended or microbial contaminants. Modern landfills are designed to contain the leachate for collection and later treatment.

Figure 50 depicts the measures that ensure surface water and groundwater are managed individually in each containment unit within the landfill in order to minimize the amount of liquid entering the leachate collection system. Environmentally engineered landfill systems generally consist of a 5-layered containment unit placed over an already impervious clay-based deposit. A landfill site consists of multiple containment units placed side-by-side (Figure 51). This containment system utilizes two liners alternating with two leachate collection systems, all capped by a protective clay layer to minimize the possibility of leachates leaving the site other than by design (Figure 52).

The primary liner is a 2 mm thick high density polyethylene plastic, known as

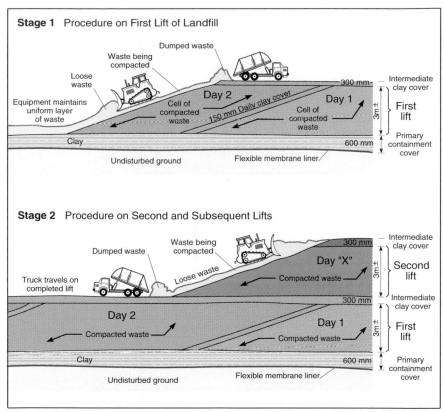

Stage 1 Procedure on First Lift of Landfill

Stage 2 Procedure on Second and Subsequent Lifts

Figure 49. Method of placing solid waste in a modern landfill *(modified from Edmonton Environmental Services)*.

a geomembrane. This plastic liner is protected on both sides by a thick fabric filter to prevent punctures by direct contact with sharp angular crushed gravel. The underlying secondary liner is a one-metre thick compacted clay layer acting as a barrier to prevent any leachate that may have escaped the primary liner. Leakages through the primary geomembrane liner can occur if the plastic liner is punctured by machines, sharp waste debris, has faulty seams where plastic sheets are joined, or is degraded by the leachate or biological activity.

Leakages through the secondary clay liner can result from a variety of causes:

cracking due to dehydration shrinkage or subsidence of the underlying support material; chemical alteration; erosion by wind or runoff; inadequate initial compaction or moisture content due to improper construction techniques; frost lens heaving; groundwater movement through the clay; slope instability associated with landslides; or disturbance of the clay by heavy equipment or vegetation roots.

Fluid collection systems above each liner intercept leachate that may have worked its way through. These collection systems generally consist of a series of drain pipes within a bed of washed gravel. These pipes ensure

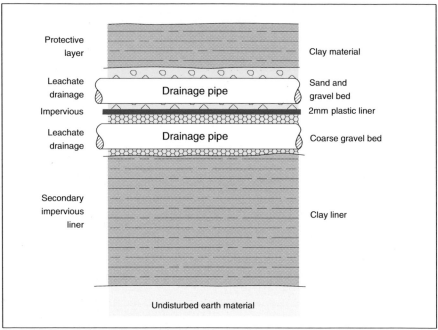

Figure 50. **Method of controlling precipitation and leachate in a modern landfill containment unit** *(modified from Edmonton Environmental Services).*

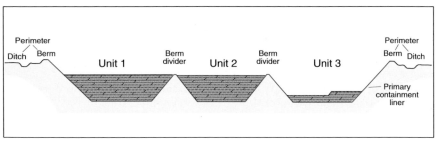

Figure 51. **Use of multiple containment units with intervening berms** *(modified from Edmonton Environmental Services).*

rapid drainage of leachate to a collection point where it can be removed for treatment.

If both liner systems should fail, modern landfills have an additional safety feature to ensure that groundwater is not contaminated. A network of groundwater monitoring

wells is installed both within and around the perimeter of the landfill site. Samples of groundwater are periodically collected from these wells to check the water quality. These samples also check on the performance of the containment liners for each

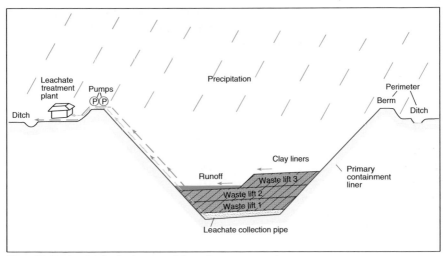

Figure 52. Design details of primary containment liner and leachate collection systems for a modern landfill *(modified from Edmonton Environmental Services)*.

landfill cell. If leachate leaks from the landfill site it can be pumped out of the ground through the monitoring wells before it circulates in the groundwater system.

The decomposition of organic matter, especially in stagnant water, generates gases in landfills. Methane and carbon dioxide are the most abundant and can be serious public health risks. Methane (marsh gas), a colourless, odourless gas, is of most concern because it is inflammable and explosive at concentrations between 5 and 13 percent in air. Being lighter than air, methane will migrate upward through the clay cap, or move laterally to be trapped in confined spaces such as underground utility corridors. Explosions and fire have occurred in some cities as a result of methane concentration in buildings constructed over old landfills. Because methane generation can continue for 30 years or more after the closing of a landfill site, long-term gas monitoring and management is required for buildings situated over or near a landfill.

The City of Edmonton has an innovative method for managing the methane gas generated at the Clover Bar site. A series of shallow wells drilled into the landfill use perforated pipes to capture and divert the methane gas to a collection station where it is filtered (scrubbed) and compressed (Figure 53). The compressed methane piped to the Clover Bar power plant is mixed with natural gas and burned in the production of steam. The steam turbine generates enough electricity to supply more than 6000 homes with power. At full capacity, it is anticipated that this landfill will generate about 200,000 cubic metres of gas each day, enough to supply 13,000 homes with power.

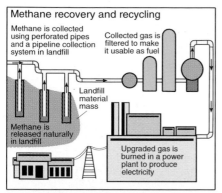

Methane recovery and recycling

Methane is collected using perforated pipes and a pipeline collection system in landfill

Collected gas is filtered to make it usable as fuel

Landfill material mass

Methane is released naturally in landfill

Upgraded gas is burned in a power plant to produce electricity

Figure 53. City of Edmonton landfill methane recovery and recycling at Clover Bar Landfill Site (modified from Edmonton Power and Edmonton Journal).

Uneven settling of the landfill surface occurs as waste material compacts and decomposes. If the landfill material is mostly domestic refuse, the settlement of a 15 m thick landfill can be as much as 1 m during a 10-year period. Severe, uneven settlement of the reclaimed landfill causes cracks in the overlying structures, roads or buildings. These cracks can provide passageway for trapped gases with possible negative safety and environmental consequences.

Natural Suitability of a Landfill Site

Certain sites have natural attributes that make them more suitable for landfill use. Others, for example abandoned gravel pits, are no longer acceptable because of the high risk in attempting to contain liquid pollutants within very permeable granular materials.

The City of Edmonton has been in the process of locating a new landfill site. While decisions in the past were strongly influenced by social or economic factors, the current selection process has a strong environmental focus, favouring sites with the most suitable natural hydrogeological conditions.

Alberta Environment has established stringent guidelines for new industrial landfills. These guidelines ensure that surface water and groundwater are not polluted by the landfill. If these environmental guidelines had been applied to Edmonton's historic landfill sites, it is likely that most, if not all, of the sites would have been rejected.

Topographic and geological conditions are evaluated to determine the natural suitability of a potential site. Areas of steep topography are unsuitable because slope movement could expose waste at the surface. Ravines, gullies, wetlands, river terraces and flood plains are also unfavourable because of typically high water tables making the site wet and difficult to operate. A high water table may also be a source of water seepage at the site and could produce leachate in the bottom of the landfill. It is important not to locate landfills next to a river where a major flood could erode protective dykes and carry waste downstream. Other features for consideration within a 500 m radius of the landfill are surface water bodies and domestic water wells. Accidental release of leachates by runoff or subsurface seepage could contaminate both surface water and groundwater.

Certain geological materials are naturally suited for a landfill site. The most favoured are impervious clayey sediments and rock such as

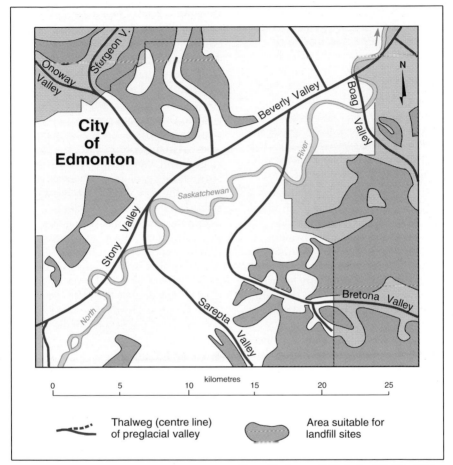

kilometres

| 0 | 5 | 10 | 15 | 20 | 25 |

— - ·· · Thalweg (centre line)
of preglacial valley

Area suitable for
landfill sites

Figure 54. Areas suitable for landfill sites. Areas floored by preglacial buried valleys are unsuitable (source: Alberta Research Council).

glaciolacustrine clay, glacial till and shale. These materials have very low seepage rates and therefore do not readily allow liquids to enter or leave. At least 15 m of undisturbed clayey sediment are required beneath a landfill to make the site most desirable. Figure 54 outlines areas around Edmonton which meet these geological criteria. The least desirable conditions are highly permeable sand and gravel

sediments which allow liquids to drain easily from a site. Sand and gravel deposits in the Edmonton area include buried preglacial bedrock and drift channels, aeolian (wind-blown) sand, glaciolacustrine (glacial lake) beach sands, and recent river channel and terrace deposits of the North Saskatchewan River and its tributaries.

In the Edmonton area, major sand and gravel aquifers are found at the bottom of many of the preglacial bedrock channels, particularly the Beverly Channel (Figure 16). These buried channel aquifers are major sources of domestic water, and landfills are permitted over these channels only if a substantial thickness of low-permeable material, such as glaciolacustrine clay or till, separates the base of the landfill from the top of the aquifer.

From a hydrogeological perspective, it would be desirable to locate landfills in areas toward which groundwater flows, called closed groundwater discharge areas. In such cases the groundwater flows toward the landfill, and leachates cannot readily leave the site. Although groundwater discharge areas generally have high water tables, which increases the potential for leachate to develop at the base of the landfill, these water tables can be lowered locally by installing drainage systems.

In places it can be difficult to determine whether groundwater is flowing into or out of a site. Whereas the direction and amount of runoff is easily determined by measuring stream discharges, it is technically much more difficult and costly to determine the direction and velocity of groundwater flowing in the ground. Water flowing through an aquifer, under natural conditions, will flow from areas of high hydraulic head, or energy, toward areas of lower hydraulic head.

To measure the differences in hydraulic head, special monitoring wells are installed, called piezometers, which are completed at various depths within the aquifer. The piezometer consists of a plastic pipe with a series of very fine slots cut in the bottom 1 to 2 m. These slots permit water to seep out of the surrounding geological materials and to enter the pipe, until it reaches a stable level. The level of water is determined with a measuring tape. Piezometers completed at various locations within the aquifer will record water-levels at different elevations. From the water-level information, it is possible to calculate the direction and path that groundwater and any fluid pollutant will travel beneath the site.

■ Ground Controls

These overviews of slope movements, floods and construction show that geology imposes controls on the urban activities that can be economically carried out at specific sites. If we break the ground rules, knowingly or unknowingly, there will be consequences and penalties, now or in the future. We have gradually discovered some of the rules, others await further exploration and enquiry.

5 GEOLOGY FOR VIEWING

River Valley Trails

John Shaw and John D. Godfrey

Until this point, the geological history of Edmonton has been described, interpreted and illustrated to help us picture the sequence and nature of the events. Yet something vital to geology is still lacking; the experience thus far has all been second hand. It is one thing to examine a photograph of the Gwynne Outlet, but quite another to stand on the valley rim and picture the torrent of glacial meltwater that carved out this impressive trench.

You now have the opportunity to experience the thrill of field observation and perhaps to open the eyes of experts with your own interpretation; indeed, Earth science has a wonderful amateur tradition! Field sites and vistas are described here along the trails in the North Saskatchewan River valley, extending from Emily Murphy Park in the west to Rundle Park in the east. This guide follows the trails from west to east, but the selected sites may be visited individually or in any sequence. All viewpoints and sites of interest are marked on a map of the river valley (Figure 55).

■ Site 1. Groat Bridge vantage point

Looking east from the Groat Bridge toward the High Level Bridge the view is dominated by the North Saskatchewan River and its valley (Figure 56). The left-hand bank of the river bounds a broad segment of the flood plain, equivalent to the lowest terrace which, in conjunction with the adjacent valley wall, makes an excellent site for Victoria Golf Course and Park (Figure 57).

The south-facing valley wall is a relatively dry environment, unable to sustain thick stands of trees. Grass, low bushes and shrubs dominate, with only scattered stands of trees. By contrast, the north-facing slopes are shaded from the sun and are thickly wooded, with aspen and spruce dominating.

The right-hand valley wall lies at the outside of the bend and has been prone to failure because of river erosion at the toe of the slope. Recent bank protection, using coarse gravel as a "rip-rap" should reduce this erosion. As well, the river appears to be responding to dam control upstream from Edmonton. While the Big Horn Dam reduces the flood peaks on the trunk stream, the tributaries downstream from the dam still flood and carry large quantities of sediment. A delicate balance that had evolved naturally over several thousand years has now been disturbed. The newly controlled North Saskatchewan River cannot transport this sediment away and it is less likely to overtop its banks in flood condition.

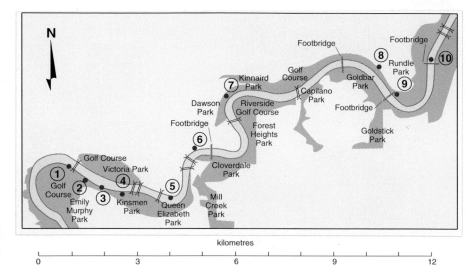

N

Footbridge
Footbridge
⑧
Rundle
Park
⑩
Golf
Kinnaird
Course
Goldbar
⑨
⑦ Park
Capilano
Park
Dawson
Riverside
Park
Park
Golf Course
Footbridge
Footbridge
Forest
Goldstick
⑥
Heights
Park
Park
Golf Course
Cloverdale
Victoria Park
Park
①
Golf ②
④
⑤
Course
Emily ③ Kinsmen
Mill
Murphy Park Queen
Creek
Park Elizabeth
Park
Park

kilometres

0   3   6   9   12

Figure 55. Location of descriptive sites along the North Saskatchewan River valley trail.

As a consequence, sediment now resides in channel bars. The upstream sediment bars along both sides of the river and a number of new sand bars along the Edmonton reach of the river are testament to this process. Strangely enough, the dam which now reduces flooding may, in the long run, compound the problem and induce flooding. Additional sediment now in the channel will reduce flow capacity, and high discharges generated by heavy rainfall downstream from the dam may cause flooding more severe than before the dam was built.

The sediment bars are quickly colonized by vegetation, horsetails followed by willows, which serve to trap more sediment and promote the growth of the bars. This "feedback" between aquatic vegetation and geomorphology illustrates the interdependence of biological and geological processes.

■ Site 2. Emily Murphy Park - slopes on the move

The steep valley wall at the east end of Emily Murphy Park is an excellent place to observe the effects of slope failure. Climb the slope by any one of the small paths through the trees and note the buff to yellow silty clay exposed by erosion. This silty clay is Glacial Lake Edmonton sediment originating near the top of the valley wall. The slope levels off at about 20 m above the river and in places even slopes away from the river channel. The valley wall has one or two distinct steps. The higher second step is separated from the valley wall by an elongate depression parallel to the wall. These steps are formed by slump blocks that slid toward the river along failure planes passing through the weak bedrock and overlying soft

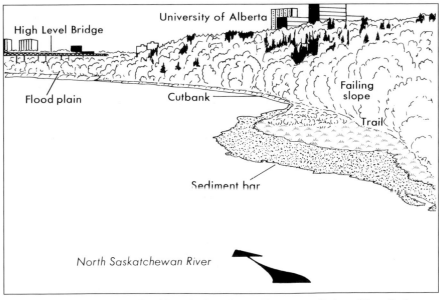

High Level Bridge

University of Alberta

Flood plain

Cutbank

Failing slope

Trail

Sediment bar

North Saskatchewan River

Figure 56. Looking downstream (east) from the Groat Bridge. The steep south slope of the valley is unstable and tree cover hides numerous landslide blocks. Sediment stored in the river channel forms a prominent bar. In the distance, the flood plain at Kinsmen Park is visible below the High Level Bridge.

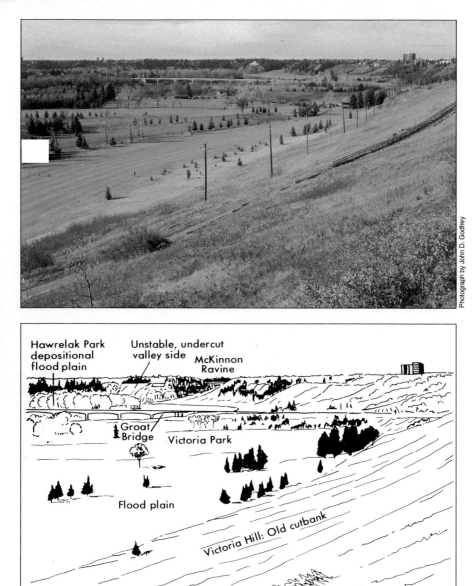

Photograph by John D. Godfrey

Figure 57. Looking west from the Le Marchand Building across Victoria Park toward the Groat Bridge. The river previously flowed directly below what is now Victoria Hill and undercut the valley wall. The channel has migrated southward, depositing material against the north bank and eroding sediments at the south valley wall. The level flood plain of Victoria Park resulted from this deposition. Upstream, the balance between erosion and deposition is seen in the extensive flood plain at William Hawrelak Park and the current erosion on the opposite side of the river near McKinnon Ravine. The grassy slopes of the drier south-facing side of the valley at Victoria Hill contrast with the thickly treed area below the University (Figure 56).

Figure 58. One of many curved tree trunks in Emily Murphy Park responding to slow surface soil creep. By contrast younger trees are straight, indicating a more stable slope in recent time.

sediments (Figure 14). The silty clay exposed along the footpaths forms the upper bed of these slump blocks.

As you return to the park, note that many trees have exposed roots, especially on the downslope side. This feature illustrates continuing soil erosion as rainwater and snowmelt run-off wash away the ground surface. Note also that the trunks of many trees are curved, angling downslope near the ground, then rising vertically (Figure 58). This condition reflects the response of trees to slow downhill soil creep which tends to tilt them downslope. Trees are programmed by nature to grow vertically, and curved trunks are simply a record of trees

straightening themselves out. They are also a record of a very slow process that might be otherwise difficult to detect.

Continue along the river path to the fenced-off area below the University. Springs are common here, about 10 m above the river. They are probably fed by groundwater flowing in the sands and gravels of the Empress Formation and emerging at the junction of the sands and the underlying, less pervious shale and sandstone of the Cretaceous bedrock.

■ Site 3. Coal Seam

Coal in the Cretaceous Horseshoe Canyon Formation is exposed halfway between Emily Murphy Park and Kinsmen Park (Figure 59). The seam is somewhat overgrown and could easily be missed. The coal seam has blocky

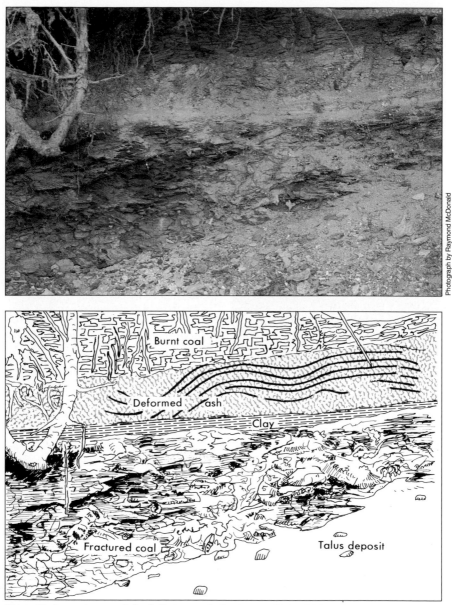

Photograph by Raymond McDonald

Figure 59. A complex association in Cretaceous bedrock strata. A 0.9 m high exposure shows a highly fractured coal seam resting on sandstone (obscured by talus) and overlain by a 2 cm thick light coloured clay bed. All of these deposits were related to the flood plain-channel environment of an ancient, swampy river. The overlying coal ignited and burnt in place in more recent time. Local slippage on the clay may have caused deformation of the shaly ash.

fractures and is about 2 m thick. It rests on an irregular surface cut into sandstone, probably having been formed in the bed of an abandoned Cretaceous river channel. Toward the top of the seam the coal has burnt in place whilst underground, leaving an orange ash with coal intact above. Coal is formed by the transformation of compressed remains of plants that grew, died and were preserved in a river swamp. The underlying sand was probably deposited in one of many channels winding through a forested swamp.

The coal is overlain by a buff-coloured mixture of clay, silt, sand and stones with streaked-out blocks of coal. This so-called colluvium is formed by the same creep processes that cause trees to bend their trunks. Additional exposures of the coal seam 12 m west and 8 m east show it to have a gentle (5°) dip eastward; i.e. contrary to the regional southwest dip. Perhaps a local gentle flexure, or a slump block rotation accounts for this reverse dip. If you are lucky, you may find a small fragment of amber (fossil resin) around these coaliferous Cretaceous strata.

Continue east of the University water intake (fenced-off buildings) toward Walterdale Flats (situated on the lowest terrace and flood plain). Flood plain sediments are well exposed along the river bank just upstream from the LRT bridge and can be reached by way of a broad ramp where the bank has been cut down and gently graded for easy access.

■ Site 4. Channel migration, flood plain overbank deposits and Mazama Ash

The pedway beneath the LRT tracks is an excellent place from which to watch the river at work (Figure 60). The swirling currents *erode* rock and sediment at the southern bank. From time to time, this undercut bank collapses into the river, sediment is swept away, and roots are left exposed (Figure 61 upper). The north bank relates a very different story. Sediment is *deposited* on a point bar along the inside of the river bend (Figure 61, lower). Horsetails, which have colonized the bar, cause deposition of fine-grained sediment on its surface. In this way the bar grows upward. As the channel migrates southward, this bar will eventually be buried by overbank flood deposits of silt and clay building up a broadening and accreting flood plain.

Nearly 4 m of flood plain sediments, built by this "vertical accretion" process, are exposed along a steep cutbank (Figure 62). Individual flood deposits are easily recognized as couplets: buried soils which represent lengthy periods between floods are separated by thick (about 25 cm) beds of silt, each deposited rapidly by a single flood. Silt from the 1915 flood is clearly visible below the modern soil. Altogether, about 15 flood deposit – soil sequences are exposed in this section.

White Mazama Ash, from the eruption of Mount Mazama, Oregon, about 6800 years ago, is prominent (Figure 63) and even stands out when this section of

Photograph by John D. Godfrey

Figure 60. Upwelling boils (smooth zones) and diving sinks between boils (rough surface with small vortices or whirlpools) illustrate the powerful turbulence of the North Saskatchewan River. View is about 2 m across in the photograph.

grey flood plain silts is viewed just upstream from the LRT bridge (Figure 62). The ash layer pinches and swells, suggesting that it was quickly reworked and redistributed by surface wash after settling through the air.

Bison bones and pieces of wood occasionally protrude from the face as it wears back. These organic debris date back as far as 8000 years BP, attesting to the relatively slow downcutting of the river.

Industrial artifacts in the more recent deposits of this section indicate that Walterdale Flats was once home to a thriving industrial complex. Bricks are strewn about the surface and some were dumped into a gully near the eastern end of the section. The gully was later filled with colluvium or dumped flood plain deposits. The section is capped with the latest flood plain silt and modern soil.

A geologist, like Sherlock Holmes, can make the following deductions from this stratigraphy. The bricks are made of local clay, and old pits on the flood plain suggest that this clay was deposited in still waters on the flood plain. The nearby abandoned Strathcona coal mine (located on the valley wall above the Pitch and Putt golf course at Kinsmen, Figure 22) could have provided coal for firing the bricks. The last flood plain silt layer (1915) shows that the bricks were manufactured before the last major flood. A historian would tell of the Pollard brothers (Chapter 3) who manufactured bricks at this site from river clays between 1898 and 1913, and

Figure 61. Complementary erosion and deposition on opposite banks of the river.

Upper: The river channel erodes the south bank as the channel migrates southward. 'Drunken' trees indicate undercut unstable slopes with soil slippage.

Lower: Deposition against the north bank eventually widens the flood plain as sand, silt and clay cover the new gravel bar.

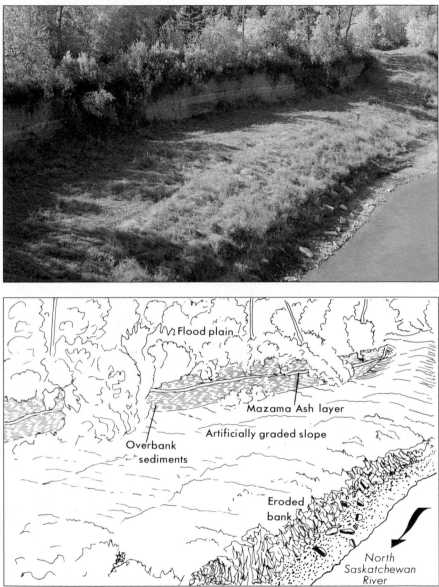

Photograph by Raymond McDonald

Figure 62. Flood plain and overbank deposits just upstream from the LRT Bridge at the south bank of the river . Overbank sediment is deposited only during floods and contains the smaller particles carried in suspension. The sand, silt and clay of these sediments contrast with the much coarser channel bed gravel. The darker layers are buried soils which formed by weathering between floods. The uppermost prominent white band is volcanic ash wind-blown from Mount Mazama, Oregon, which erupted explosively about 6800 B.P.

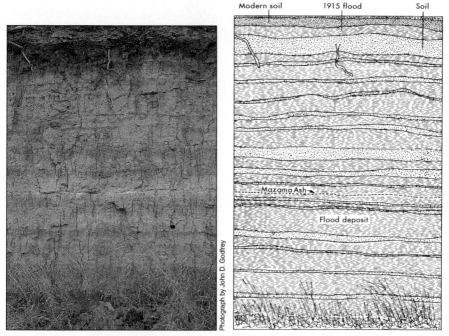

Modern soil   1915 flood   Soil

Mazama Ash

Flood deposit

Figure 63. Silty clay flood deposits (light) alternate with soils (dark) in a 3.33 m high exposure of flood plain sediment. The buried soils have been compressed and oxidized and are much thinner than the modern soils. The white Mazama Ash (approximately 1 cm thick) stands out clearly.

how the plant closed after the major flood of 1915.

Continue eastward to the John Walter Museum which holds a wealth of information on this entrepreneur from the Orkneys. He built boats, ran a lumber mill and general store, and operated ferries. He grew rich by the river and was made poor by it, never recovering from the financial ruin of the 1915 flood. Photographs in the museum and at the entrance show the smoky industrial complex on the flood plain and the devastation of the great flood. Unfortunately, the flood-lines between the lintels and upstairs windows on the old log buildings have been painted over.

Cross 105 Street beneath the bridge and then cross the river on the pedestrian path on the east side of the bridge. From the bridge deck note that the strongest river current crosses from the north to the south bank, switching the locations of erosion and deposition. The small community of Lavigne is perched precariously above the eroded south bank, probably on a terrace remnant. The Rossdale flats on the opposite bank record deposition over several thousands of years. The Rossdale generating station, John Ducey baseball stadium, and fashionable, modern homes, while safe from any immediate danger of bank erosion, nonetheless appear at risk from flooding.

Continue along the path (it is usually open) between the generating station and the river bank and stop on the small grassy knoll beyond the footbridge overlooking the boatlaunch ramp.

■ Site 5. Eroded valley wall at Lavigne (Skunk Hollow)

The valley wall across the river and upstream from the grassy knoll is thickly treed (Figure 64). The dominance of spruce indicates that this shaded slope has a Boreal Forest microclimate. Recent, shallow slope failures have sliced slide scars through the forest and piled jumbled trees and earth over the undercut bank. In time, the river will remove this debris to complete another small increment of slope retreat.

The lower part of the slope, downstream from Lavigne and across the river from the knoll, exposes bare or sparsely vegetated bedrock (Figure 65). Constant undercutting by the river and slope erosion make it difficult for soils and plants to take hold here. Deep gullies in the bedrock became truncated as the river cut back into the valley wall. These gullies are now infilled with light coloured colluvium derived from the glacial deposits on the slopes above.

Continue along the riverside trail skirting around Rossdale. Note the expensive houses with lower floors well below flood level; homeowners here must sign a waiver releasing the city from responsibility for flood damage, basements are rare, and most furnaces are above ground.

Pass under the James McDonald Bridge, built at another river current cross-over, where the Rossdale flats end and the Cloverdale flats begin on the opposite side of the river. The Muttart Conservatory pyramids are built on a slip-off slope marking the positions of the shifting channel as the river had simultaneously cut downward and laterally. As we might expect, erosion replaces deposition on the north bank, downstream from the James McDonald Bridge.

■ Site 6. Grierson Park - a war zone

This park, with its smoothly graded slopes, belies an expensive battle between City development and nature, which had a little help from coal mining. This historic landslide slope is described in Chapter 4. The whole hillslope has been on the move as indicated by the large amphitheatre bounded by a slide scar at the headwall of a huge landslide (Figures 66 and 38). Several factors contributed to the slope instability: river undercutting steepened the bank; the bedrock at river level in the vicinity of the slide contains weak bentonitic shale; and coal mining caused stress release which further weakened the rock. Subsidence also occurs as old mine adits and shafts collapse. Not surprisingly, maintenance of the road on Grierson Hill has been a constant chore and the unstable slopes have added considerably to the cost of the Edmonton Convention Centre.

Recent engineering modifications of the river and valley wall are on a grand scale. The slopes are graded and have

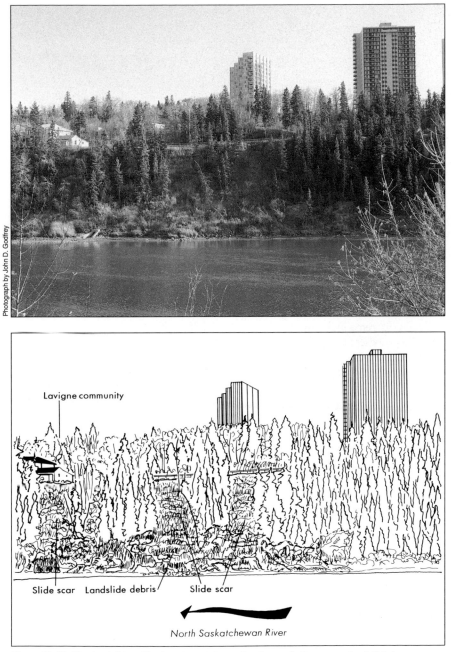

Figure 64. Shallow landslides at Lavigne have cut prominent scars in the spruce stand. Debris accumulating at the foot of the slope is being eroded by the river.

Photograph by John D. Godfrey

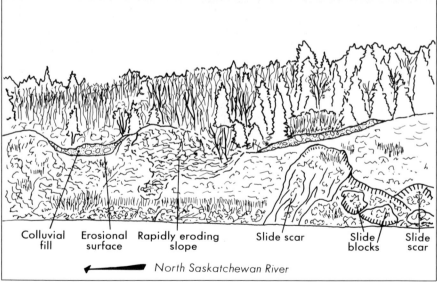

Colluvial fill   Erosional surface   Rapidly eroding slope   Slide scar   Slide blocks   Slide scar

North Saskatchewan River

Figure 65. The river is actively eroding the south valley wall just east of Lavigne. Repetitive shallow slides prevent trees from taking hold and the bare soil is susceptible to erosion by rills. A sign of progressive rapid erosion is the exposure of colluvium in small tributary gullies truncated upslope as the river cuts laterally.

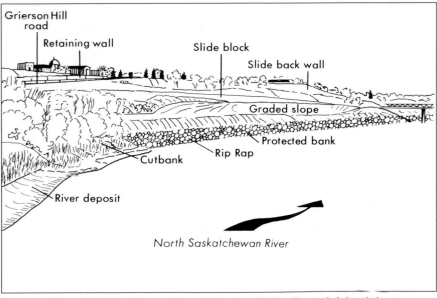

Figure 66. Grierson Park viewed eastward from the Low Level Bridge. The graded slope below Edmonton Convention Centre parking lot and the retaining wall atop Grierson Hill mark attempt to control natural processes. For a while at least, the river will not be able to undercut and steepen the outside bank and the valley slope should be stable. The new park covers only part of the large slide below the slide scar. (For further detail see Figure 38.)

been extended toward the river to reduce their gradient. The toe of the slope is protected against river erosion by an enormous bank of glacial erratics, a further legacy of the Laurentide Ice Sheet (Figure 67), and the steepest part of the slope is held in place by a sturdy retaining wall. What will the river do next?

Follow the bicycle path through Riverdale, a flood plain community like Rossdale, though with more of a mix of older and newer houses. Continue beneath the Dawson Bridge where the river current crosses over to erode the north bank in Dawson Park and Kinnaird Park. It is no coincidence that the bridges are commonly at river current cross-overs: the channel is more

Figure 67. Grierson Park bank protection. Huge boulders delivered by the Laurentide Ice Sheet are used as rip-rap to protect the bank against river erosion.

stable there and less prone to scouring of the bank and bed, and access to the valley floor is easier in the absence of the steep, undercut valley slopes around the outside of bends.

■ Site 7. Dawson Park - Cretaceous bedrock and glacial sediment

One of the best exposed and most interesting geological sections in Edmonton is the bedrock and glacial sediment at the outside of the riverbend near the east end of Dawson Park. A combination of undercutting by the river and relatively resistant bedrock have resulted in a steep cliff face (Figure 68).

The Cretaceous bedrock here is mainly sandstone: the cleaner sands are light grey and the more muddy (clayey) beds are darker grey. Some of the cleaner sands are well cemented and

Photograph by John D. Godfrey

Figure 68. Cretaceous bedrock at Dawson Park consists of interfingering shale and sandstone beds. The sands were originally deposited in river channels by strong currents and the finer grained muds were deposited on broad mudbanks by gentler currents. Exposure is 4 to 5 m high.

stand out from the face in prominent shelves. These clean sands are cross-bedded, and sets of steeply inclined beds represent the migrating faces of sand waves or river bed dunes a few tens of centimetres high (Figure 69). These dunes were probably formed by river currents and the sandstone is most likely a channel deposit. The shales at Grierson Park were deposited on mudflats and we can imagine the Cretaceous-age scenery with deep, sediment-laden rivers meandering through submerged mudflats. Volcanic eruptions to the west darkened the skies with ash which settled through the air to be deposited in the muds. The bentonitic component

125

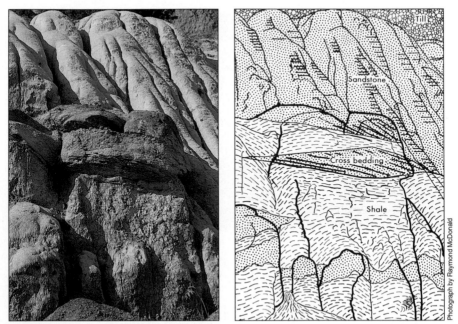

Photograph by Raymond McDonald

Figure 69. Dawson Park. Cross-bedding (about 30 cm thick) in coarser-grained sandstone represents dunes or large ripples created by strong currents in the ancient river channel. As dunes migrate downstream, layers of various grain size are deposited and preserved on the steep downstream (lee) face. These bedding structures are called cross-beds.

of the sands and mud is a weathering product of the volcanic ash (Figure 70). Bentonitic muds expand to about ten times their dry volume upon wetting. As the muds dry, they shrink and crack, forming a characteristic "popcorn texture" at the surface.

The sand also contains flecks of coaly organic matter and passes upward into a thick coal seam. The coal marks the abandonment of the channel and the accumulation of organic debris in a backswamp beyond the direct influence of the channelized flow. These swamps, unlike those where mud was deposited, must have been thickly vegetated and were probably relatively shallow.

The coal, formed 65 million years ago in the Cretaceous Period, is overlain directly by glacial till deposited about 20,000 years ago during the late Wisconsin Ice Age. There is simply no record at this location of the intervening millions of years, i.e. there is a gap of unrecorded geological time. However, it is probable that erosion during the Tertiary Period and early stages of the glacial advance has stripped away the immediately preceding Cretaceous deposits.

Photograph by Raymond McDonald

Figure 70. Dawson Park. "Popcorn texture" forms on the surface of shales containing swelling clay. Exposure is about 1 m wide in photograph.

Till is a homogeneous mixture of clay, silt and sand, with occasional pebbles and large boulders. Erratics from the Canadian Shield (including granite, gneiss and Athabasca sandstone) are plentiful. These boulders were polished and striated in the course of glacial transport. Clean looking, washed sand lenses near the base of the till were deposited by subglacial streams draining meltwater at the bed of the ice sheet. Vertical joints in the till formed by shrinkage as the initially water-logged sediment dried out.

Highly convoluted sediment above the glacial deposits contains till and Glacial Lake Edmonton silty clay mixed together and locally compressed into contorted bands. Once moved, these materials are called *colluvium*, produced by downslope creep which mixes sedimentary beds from higher upslope.

The sandstone is also susceptible to erosion by running water. Deep rills result from erosion of the steep faces. Rill formation is guided by steep fracture zones in the bedrock. The more

resistant clay ironstones and well-cemented channel sands typically form caps protecting underlying columns of softer sandstone: it is not necessary to travel to Drumheller to see the badlands and hoodoo landscape (Figure 71)!

Continue through Kinnaird Park noting the prominent slide blocks containing intact lacustrine sediment which have moved downslope by gravity. Poorly exposed bedrock along the trail just west of Kinnaird Ravine is weak, bentonitic shale. Weak, impervious shaly bedrock at the base of slopes is common to many landslide areas.

A large, recently formed sand bar splits the channel just upstream of the Capilano Bridge. The willows established along the bar top indicate that it is a relatively stable river channel feature.

The bicycle trail climbs above the Highlands Golf Course and continues eastward along Ada Boulevard.

■ Site 8. Valley viewpoint from Ada Boulevard at 108th Avenue

This point affords an excellent overview of some of the major landforms in the river valley (Figure 72). Erosion on the outside of the river bend has undercut and steepened the north wall of the valley. The wide flood plain below the south wall of the valley represents a long period of lateral cutting by the river during which time there was little downcutting. By contrast, the slip-off slope above the flood plain tracks the path of the channel in the early stages of valley formation when the river cut both sideways and downward.

Continue eastward into Rundle Park, to the collection of glacial erratic boulders near the trail entrance at the west end (Figure 73).

■ Site 9. Rundle Park

Thirteen glacial erratics collected from within the City have been assembled around the Trail House (Figures 73 and 74). All of these boulders are sufficiently large not to have undergone lengthy stream transport; they are without question glacial erratics. They were shaped by glacial processes with only slight, subsequent rounding in meltwater streams. Other postglacial modifications of shape reflect either natural weathering or handling by heavy equipment in the course of excavation and site placement. Heavy equipment handling has led to bruise marks along edges, rusty metallic scrape marks and occasional split faces along joint and bedding planes of the weaker soft sandstones.

Very commonly, the transport of rock fragments, whether the agent is water, ice, wind or downslope mass movement, leaves telltale clues. For example, boulders from glaciers are likely to be polished and striated; boulders, cobbles and sand transported in streams become rounded; and wind-blown sand grains are commonly rounded and "frosted" (due to very small-scale abrasion pitting).

Although the last part of their journey was on the back of a city truck, these erratics had already travelled considerable distances in the Laurentide Ice Sheet. Only the toughest

Photograph by Raymond McDonald

Figure 71. Dawson Park. Incipient hoodoos forming beneath resistant caps of iron-cemented sandstone. The resistant caps divert surface run-off and protect the hoodoos from erosion. The hoodoos are about 3 metres tall.

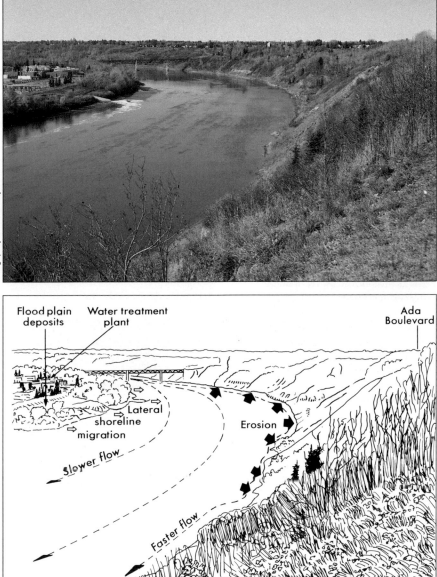

Figure 72. This view westward from Ada Boulevard illustrates various aspects of river valley development. Deposition on the inside of the bend has created the flood plain. Below Capilano Bridge the fastest flowing river current "crosses over" the channel and impinges on the outside of the bend below Ada Boulevard. The steep valley wall and sparse vegetation reflect undercutting and slope failure. As complementary erosion and deposition progress on opposite sides of the river, the valley is widened and the active channel becomes more sinuous.

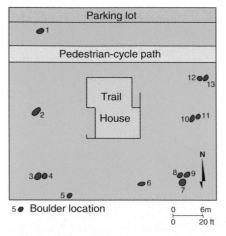

Figure 73. Rundle Park, plan of 13 erratic boulders at Trail House.

of rocks, like granite and gneiss, could have survived the longer journey from the Hudson Bay region to Edmonton.

The group of erratic boulders includes: two Cretaceous sandstones; one Paleozoic limestone/dolostone; two Precambrian Athabasca Group sandstones; and a combination of eight Precambrian Shield metamorphic gneisses and granites. The bedrock sources of these rocks tell of the flow path of the continental ice sheet into the Edmonton region. They show that the ice sheet started from the general region of Hudson Bay (Figure 9) and, along the way, this continental ice sheet sequentially eroded:

Figure 74. Rundle Park, Trail House at west end. Looking northwest from side of trail and parking lot. Glacial erratic boulder groups of #10, #11, and #12, 13 in foreground, and Rundle - Gold Bar Parks footbridge in the background..

• hard gneisses and granites exposed in the Canadian Shield, west of Hudson Bay, 750 to 1250 km away from Edmonton; *(the ice sheet then flowed southwesterly)*.

• hard Athabasca sandstone in extreme northern Saskatchewan, 450 to 750 km away from Edmonton; *(the ice sheet then flowed southwestward, entering Alberta east of Fort McMurray.)*

• soft but durable limestone/dolostone from the Alberta/Saskatchewan border area, 400 km away from Edmonton; *(the ice sheet then flowed in a more southerly path over the Alberta plains).*

•soft Cretaceous sandstone from less than 400 km away, perhaps from the Fort McMurray area; *(the continental ice sheet continued to flow southward into northern U.S.A.).*

Boulder #1: Cretaceous sandstone.
Boulder #2: Devonian(?) limestone/dolostone.
Boulder #3: Precambrian gneissic red granite.
Boulder #4: Precambrian foliated white granite.
Boulder #5: Precambrian Athabasca Group sandstone.
Boulder #6: Precambrian metasedimentary gneiss.
Boulder #7: Cretaceous sandstone.
Boulder #8: Precambrian Athabasca Group sandstone.
Boulder #9: Precambrian gneissic granitoid.
Boulder #10: Precambrian red granite gneiss.
Boulder #11: Precambrian dark gneiss.
Boulder #12: Precambrian gneissoid light red granite.

Boulder #13: Precambrian red feldspar augen gneiss.

Fluvial features and well-exposed bedrock at Rundle Park illustrate the work of past and present rivers. Bedrock exposed just upstream of the Rundle - Gold Bar Parks footbridge exhibits all of the major components of the Horseshoe Canyon Formation: sandstone, shale, and coal seams (Figure 75). Shale separates two thick sandstone units and there are two prominent coal seams. The two sandstone beds were probably deposited in migrating river channels, while deposition of the finer-grained clays took place on submerged interchannel flood plains to produce the shales. In some respects, this sedimentation pattern is similar to the depositional sequences of a modern river: the coarser-grained sand and gravel deposits of the channel are capped by fine-grained flood plain deposits as the river migrates laterally and periodically floods. This fining-upward sequence, as it is called, is typical of meandering stream deposits. However, the gravels and silts of the modern sediments are coarser than the corresponding sands and clays of the Cretaceous beds. This contrast indicates a steeper gradient and faster flow for the modern river compared to its Cretaceous counterpart.

As well, the modern stream does not accumulate thick organic beds, partly because it is in a downcutting cycle, unlike the Cretaceous streams which built thick sediment accumulations. Coal seams in the Cretaceous rocks represent almost pure accumulations of

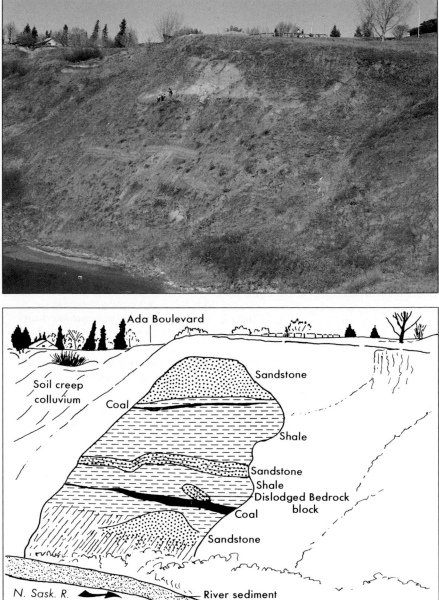

Figure 75. Rundle Park. Cretaceous bedrock strata exposed in the north bank, west of the Gold Bar - Rundle Parks footbridge. This succession is typical of river deposits, where each sediment type accumulates in a sub-environment of the river valley. The vertical alternation of beds indicates channel migration across the valley floor together with a shift of sub-environments. This exposure appears to record three periods when the channel occupied this site.

Photograph by John D. Godfrey

Figure 76. Rundle Park. At the east side of the south end of the Rundle - Gold Bar Parks footbridge, a tributary delta is building into the North Saskatchewan River. Such deltas result from the absence of flood peaks in the main river channel, as a result of construction of the Big Horn Dam upstream.

plant debris in luxuriantly vegetated riverine swamps. About 10 m of compressed plant fibre are needed for transformation to 1 m of coal.

The effects of the Big Horn Dam on the depositional regime of the modern river are well illustrated at Rundle Park. Just downstream of the Rundle - Gold Bar Parks footbridge, a small, right-bank tributary is building a delta out into the North Saskatchewan River channel (Figure 76). It is most unlikely that this would have been possible without reduction of flood peaks by the Big Horn Dam upstream. This sedimentation in the channel is a consequence of human interference with the natural cycle of flow in the river. It will be interesting to monitor this depositional feature over the long term.

■ Site 10. Rundle Park - Strathcona Science Park footbridge

In-channel sediment storage has created a streamlined bar at the Rundle-Strathcona Science Park footbridge (Figure 77). The bar surface is rippled in places, showing the interaction between the river currents and its bed. These rippled bedforms, although smaller than dunes, are similar to those in the Cretaceous cross-bedded channel sandstones at Dawson Park (Figure 69). Clumps of horsetails serve to impede the current and trap sediment in their wake to promote bar growth. Willows are firmly established on the higher parts of the bar.

Photograph by John D. Godfrey

Figure 77. Streamlined bar at the Rundle Park - Strathcona Science Park footbridge. The bar accumulates at intermediate flood stages and the willows indicate that it is fairly stable. Close inspection shows how clumps of vegetation trap sediment to their lee side and promote bar accumulation. It is usual to find beautiful ripples and current ridges on the bar top which change with every flood.

FURTHER READING

■ Chapter 2

Bayrock, L.A., (1972): Surficial geology Edmonton NTS 83H; Alberta Research Council, coloured map, scale 1:250 000, with marginal notes.

Bowser, W.E., A.A. Kjearsgaard, T.W. Peters and R.E. Wells, (1962): Soil survey of the Edmonton Sheet (83-H); The University of Alberta Bulletin No. SS-4, 66 pages.

Gadd, B., (1986): Handbook of the Canadian Rockies; Corax Press, Jasper, Alberta, 875 pages.

Geological Survey of Canada, (1989 onward): Geology of Canada Series, Vols. 1 to 9, (part of Decade of North American Geology Project DNAG)

Green, R., (1972): Geological map of Alberta; Alberta Geological Survey, Alberta Research Council, coloured map, scale 1:1,267,000.

Hardy, W.G. (Editor-in-Chief), (1967): Alberta, a natural history; M.G. Hurtig, Publishers, Edmonton, Alberta, 343 pages.

Helgason, G., (1987): The first Albertans, an archeological search; Lone Pine Publishing, Edmonton, 222 pages.

Levin, H.L., (1987): The Earth through time (3rd Edition): Saunders College Publishing, New York, 593 pages.

MacGregor, J.G., (1967): Edmonton, a history; M.G. Hurtig, Publishers, Edmonton, 328 pages.

Mossop, G.D. and I. Shetsen, (compilers), (In press): Geological atlas of the Western Canada Sedimentary Basin; Calgary, Canadian Society of Petroleum Geologists and Alberta Research Council.

Nelson, S.J., (1970): The face of time, a geological history of Western Canada; Alberta Society of Petroleum Geologists, Calgary, 133 pages.

Rains, B. and J. Welch, (1988): Out-of-phase Holocene terraces in part of the North Saskatchewan River Basin, Alberta; Canadian Journal of Earth Sciences, Vol. 25, pp. 454-464.

Tarbuck, E.J, and F.K. Lutgens, (1993): The Earth, an introduction to physical geology; Macmillan Publishing Co., New York, 654 pages.

Tyrrell, J.B., (1915): Gold on the North Saskatchewan River; Transactions of the Canadian Mining Institute, Vol. 18, pp. 160-173

Whitten, D.G.A. and J.R.V. Brooks, (1987): The Penguin dictionary of geology; Penguin Books Inc., Baltimore, Maryland, 493 pages.

■ Chapter 3

Beach, H.H., (1934): The geology of the coal seams of Edmonton and district and a history of its mining development. Unpublished thesis, The University of Alberta, 148 pages.

Blower, J., (1986): Gold rush; A pictorial look at the part Edmonton played in the gold era of the 1890s; Edmonton Northlands, Edmonton, 199 pages.

Edwards, W.A.D., R.B. Hudson and D.W. Scafe, (1985): Aggregate resources of the Edmonton/Lloydminster region; Alberta Research Council, Bulletin 47, 64 pages.

Energy Resources Conservation Board, (1988): Coal mine atlas; Operating and abandoned coal mines in Alberta; Calgary, 365 pages.

Halferdahl L.B., (1965): The occurrence of gold in Alberta rivers; Alberta Research Council, Open File Report 1965-11, 22 pages.

Harben, P.W. and R.L. Bates, (1990): Industrial minerals: geology and world deposits; Metal Bulletin Plc., London, 312 pages.

Kerr, S.A., (1986): Atlantic No. 3; S.A. Kerr, Calgary, Alberta, 226 pages.

Mason, J.M., (1983): Bricks in Alberta; John M. Mason, Edmonton, 154 pages.

Schrumm, J.R., (1974): Valley of gold; Alberta Historical Review, Vol. 22, No. 4, pp. 14-25.

Shaw, R.P. and R.D. Morton, (1990): Gold mineralization in Lower Cambrian McNaughton Formation, Athabasca Pass, Central Rocky Mountains; structural, mineralogical and temporal relationships; Canadian Journal of Earth Sciences, Vol. 27, No. 4, pp. 477-493.

Taylor, R.S., (1970): Atlas: Coal-mine workings of the Edmonton area; Spence Taylor and Associates Ltd., Edmonton, Alberta, 33 pages.

Tyrrell, J.B., (1887): Report on part of Northern Alberta and portions of adjacent districts of Assiniboia and Saskatchewan; Geological Survey of Canada, Annual Report, Vol. 2, Part E, pp. 151-152.

■ Chapter 4

Alberta Environment, (1987): Guidelines for industrial landfills; Environmental Protection Services, 50 pages.

Kathol, C.P. and R.A. McPherson, (1975): Urban geology of Edmonton; Alberta Research Council, Bulletin 32, 61 pages.

Mustapha, A.M., S. Figliuzzi, H. Rickert and G. Coles, (1981): History of floods in the North Saskatchewan River Basin; Alberta Environmental Engineering Support Services, Technical Services Division, 112 pages.

Rutter, N.W. and S. Thomson, (1982): Effects of geology on the development of Edmonton, Alberta, Canada; Reviews in Engineering Geology, Vol. 5, pp. 55-62.

Samide, G.W. and S.A. Lowe, (1974): Flood plain study of the North Saskatchewan River through Edmonton; Alberta Environmental Engineering Support Services, Technical Services Division, 35 pages.

Scarfe, E., (1990): The Ground Rules; in Alberta Rebound, (A. Van Herk, editor), Newest Press, Edmonton, pp. 264-274.

GLOSSARY OF TERMS

A selection from the fields of Geology and Engineering

Modified references are made to: "Longman illustrated dictionary of geology" by Alec Watt, Longman York Press, "The Penguin dictionary of geology" by Whitten and Brooks, and "Glossary of geology" third edition by Bates and Jackson, American Geological Institute.

Aggradation - the building up of a surface by sedimentary deposition; the opposite of degradation.

Alluvium - detritus - clay, silt, sand, gravel and boulders - which has been moved and deposited by streams.

Amalgam - an alloy of mercury with one or more metals; a pasty amalgam results from the extraction of free gold by mercury.

Bearing capacity - the maximum load per unit area that the ground can safely support without failing.

Bedrock - a general term for the rock that underlies soil or other unconsolidated surficial material.

Bentonite - a soft, plastic, light coloured sedimentary rock, composed essentially of the smectite clay mineral group plus colloidal silica. Formed by chemical weathering of volcanic ash.

Chert - a dense, hard cryptocrystalline siliceous sedimentary rock, occurring as beds or nodules. Flint is a variety of chert.

Clay - (1) a *clastic particle size class* of less than 2 micrometres in diameter; (2) a group of loosely defined *silicate minerals* with a crystalline sheet structure, commonly formed by the weathering of other silicate minerals. Clay minerals commonly occur as clay- sized particles and readily take up water.

Clastic - describes sediments made up of fragments (*clasts*) produced by the break up of pre-existing rocks.

Coal - an organic readily combustible sedimentary rock, typically stratified, consisting of more than 50% by weight and more than 70% by volume of carbonaceous material. The parent materials are plant remains, similar to those in peat, which have been changed physically and chemically through geological time. Differences in kinds of plant materials, degree of metamorphism (rank) and proportion of impurities are used in the classification of coal.

Continental glacier (ice sheet) - a glacier of considerable thickness, unconfined by underlying topography, covering a large part of a continent and greater than 50,000 km^2 in area.

Dolostone - a sedimentary rock composed of the abundant mineral dolomite, calcium magnesium carbonate. The formerly used rock term "dolomite" is falling into disuse in favour of dolostone because of confusion with the *mineral dolomite*.

Drift - a mining term for a horizontal underground passage, providing access from a hillside into mine workings in a coal seam or vein of ore.

Drilling mud - a dense suspension, commonly of the swelling clay bentonite and usually in water but sometimes in oil; used in rotary drilling.

Erratic - a rock fragment (pebble to large boulder) that has been carried by glacial ice for some distance from its source then came to rest when the ice melted.

Flood plain - the relatively smooth flat land adjacent to a stream channel subject to flooding when the volume of flowing water exceeds the capacity of the stream channel. It is constructed by repeated deposition of suspended sediment in the overbank flood waters.

Fluvial - related to rivers.

Frost heave - the lifting or upward movement (commonly uneven) resulting in the general distortion of surface soils, rocks, vegetation, and structures such as pavements, due to subsurface freezing of water and pressure from the growth of ice masses.

Glacio-isostasy - refers to depression or uplift of the Earth's crust in response to loading or unloading by the addition or removal of a continental glacier.

Glaciofluvial deposits - formed by meltwater from a glacier or ice sheet, typically coarse-grained, stratified sediments largely of gravelly sand.

Gneiss - a foliated, coarse-grained, high-grade metamorphic rock characterized by alternating layers of dark- and light- coloured minerals that commonly show flow folding, i.e. typical of rock deformation under plastic conditions.

Granite - a coarse-grained, plutonic igneous rock composed of the abundant minerals potassium feldspar and quartz, usually with minor amounts of mica or amphibole. Forms by the slow-cooling of molten rock in major batholithic masses typically within the roots of folded mountain belts.

Igneous rocks - formed by cooling and consolidation from parent liquid rock (magma); the cooling can take place either rapidly as in the case of lavas in a volcanic eruption, or slowly at various depths within the crust of the Earth, as in the case of granite.

Ion - an atom that has gained or lost one or more electrons and has become electrically charged.

Kame - a hill, made of glacial deposits, typically sand and gravel, deposited by glacial meltwater, either at the surface, beneath, or at the edge of a glacier.

Karst topography - typical of limestone terrain where infiltrating surface water and groundwater dissolve the rock to form caverns, tunnels, pipes and sinkholes.

Limestone - a sedimentary rock composed predominantly of calcite, calcium carbonate. Limestone can be formed from clastic, organic or chemical constituents. The vast majority of limestones form by the evaporation of seawater in tropical regions.

Magma - rock matter in a hot molten state.

Mantle - a shell in the Earth, intermediate between the crust and the core.

Metamorphism - the processes by which rocks are changed by heat, pressure, chemical reactions or some combination of these three factors to form metamorphic rocks. The metamorphism can be expressed by changes in mineral composition, texture or structure of a pre-existing igneous, sedimentary or metamorphic rock. Changes taking place in rocks at or close to the Earth's surface (weathering or diagenesis) are not included in the term metamorphism.

Mineral - a naturally occurring substance with a definite or definite range of chemical composition, and specific physical properties and crystalline structure.

Montmorillonite - a member of the smectite group of swelling clay minerals formed typically by the weathering of volcanic ash; it is the active clay mineral in many soils of the Edmonton region.

Moraine - a landform of rock debris transported by glacial ice.

Orogeny - the process or an episode of mountain building.

Paleozoic Era - the span of geological time from 570 to 230 million years ago, i.e. the beginning of the Cambrian to the end of the Permian Periods.

Pile - a long, relatively slender structural foundation component, usually made of timber, steel, reinforced or prestressed concrete, that is driven or jetted into the ground or cast in place within a borehole.

Placer deposit - a surficial mineral deposit formed by mechanical concentration of mineral particles from weathered debris. Common types are beach placers and stream placers. Heavy minerals are usually concentrated, like magnetite, ilmenite, garnet, gold, rutile, platinum and cassiterite.

Plate (tectonic) - a portion of the Earth's surface that behaves as a single rigid structural unit. Plates are about 100 to 150 km thick. They may be made up of continental crust, oceanic crust, or both, on top of a layer of the upper mantle.

Precambrian - the span of time from the origin of the Earth to the beginning of the Cambrian Period; i.e. about 4000 million years.

Precambrian basement - a general term for Precambrian igneous and metamorphic crustal rocks which cover a wide area of a continent and on which unconformably rest sediments of later age.

Precambrian Shield - a large area of exposed Precambrian igneous and metamorphic rocks in a craton, surrounded by a sediment-covered platform.

Radiometric (age) dating - a method of determining the age of rocks and minerals by measuring the ratio of radioactive parent elements and the stable daughter elements into which they decay.

Rock - a natural material consisting of an aggregate of one or more minerals. Rocks are divided into three main classes depending on their mode of formation: igneous, sedimentary and metamorphic.

Runoff - that portion of the precipitation falling on the Earth's surface that directly reaches the stream drainage system. The remainder seeps into the ground to contribute to soil moisture and to the groundwater system.

Sandstone - a clastic arenaceous sedimentary rock consisting of fragments from 1/16 (0.0625 mm) to 2 mm in diameter. The fragments may be rounded to subrounded and are typically dominated by quartz grains.

Saturated - a condition where the connected voids of a material (e.g. rock) are filled with a liquid, usually water.

Schist - a foliated metamorphic rock of medium- to coarse-grain size, which splits easily along its *schistosity*, planes of weakness created by the parallel arrangement of platy minerals such as micas.

Sediment - in the wider sense includes any unconsolidated clastic, organic or chemical material deposited by ice, wind, mass movement, flowing or standing water. *Sedimentary* (adjective).

Shaft - an approximately vertical opening in the ground providing access from the surface down to underground mine workings; used for transporting men, supplies, rock and ore, or for ventilating underground workings.

Shale - an argillaceous, fissile, well-bedded sedimentary rock with particles less than 1/256 mm (2 micrometres) in diameter.

Slope (mining term) - an inclined opening in the ground providing access from the surface down to underground mine workings.

Stratigraphy - the study of layered rocks, their nature, occurrence, classification and interrelationships.

Stratum - (bed) (pl. strata) a layer of uniform sedimentary material that is delineated above and below by clearly marked planar surfaces.

Subcrop - a "subsurface outcrop" where an erosionally truncated rock unit is buried beneath an unconformity.

Subduction zone - a plate junction where an oceanic lithospheric plate is being forced down (subducted) below an overriding continental or oceanic plate. The "stick-slip" movement of lithospheric plates is thought to be one major cause of earthquakes.

Terrace - a long, narrow, relatively level or gently inclined surface, bounded along one edge by a steeper descending slope and along the other by a steeper ascending slope. A terrace commonly occurs along the margin and above the level of a body of water, marking a former higher water level, e.g. a stream terrace.

Thalweg - the line connecting the lowest or deepest points along a stream bed or valley, i.e. the longitudinal profile of a stream or valley.

Trilobite - an extinct class of Arthropoda. The external skeleton enclosing the back was divided into three parts. Trilobites were prolific during the Paleozoic Era.

Ultramafic - (ultrabasic) igneous rocks, commonly plutonic, composed essentially of ferromagnesian minerals.

Water table - the surface of the groundwater system below which the pore spaces of rocks and soils are filled (saturated) with water.

Weathering - the combination of processes by which rocks at or near the surface are broken up or decomposed; it includes mechanical, chemical and biological weathering. Weathering is part of the process of erosion.

APPENDIX

Compilation of professional organizations and associations, educational, research and related institutions and agencies, and suppliers of geological materials in Edmonton.

■ Professional Organizations and Associations

Association of Professional Engineers, Geologists and Geophysicists of Alberta (APEGGA)
15th Floor Scotia Place, Tower One
10060 Jasper Avenue
Edmonton, Alberta T5J 4A2
telephone (403) 426-3990
The Geotechnical Society of Edmonton, and other professional engineering groups active in tunneling and bridge design are based in Edmonton can be reached through APEGGA.

Edmonton Geological Society
c/o Department of Geology
The University of Alberta
Edmonton, Alberta T6G 2E3
telephone (403) 492-3265

Alberta Chamber of Resources
Suite 1410, 10235-101 Street, Edmonton
Alberta T5J 3G1
telephone (403) 420-1030

■ Educational, Research and Related Institutions and Agencies

Alberta Department of Environmental Protection
2nd Floor, North Petroleum Plaza
9945-108 Street
Edmonton, Alberta, T5K 2G6
telephone (403) 427-3520
Major sales and distribution centre for Provincial and Federal maps and aerial photographs.

Alberta Geological Survey
Alberta Research Council
Terrace Plaza, 7th floor, 4445 Calgary Trail South, Edmonton, Alberta
telephone (403) 438-7555
Mailing address: PO Box 8330
Edmonton Alberta, T6H 5X2
*Extensive technical library of journals and maps. The main office location houses main library, publication sales and modern laboratories and services available for contract research and development.
250 Karl Clark Road;
telephone (403) 450-5111*

The University of Alberta,
Departments of Geography, Geology,
and Soil Science

Department of Geography
The University of Alberta
Edmonton, Alberta T6G 2H4
telephone (403) 492-3274
National and international map collection
and extensive aerial photograph collection
with emphasis on Alberta.

Department of Geology
The University of Alberta
Edmonton, Alberta T6G 2E3
telephone (403) 492-3265
Extensive museum collections and displays
of minerals, rocks, fossils and ore minerals.
It houses the third largest meteorite
collection in Canada. Open to the public
during business hours by arrangement.
Telephone Geology Office: (403) 492-3265.

Department of Soil Science
The University of Alberta
Edmonton, Alberta T6G 2E3
telephone (403) 492-3242
Has a display of soil monoliths representing
all major soil types from across Canada.

Provincial Museum of Alberta
12845-102 Avenue
Edmonton, Alberta T5N 0M6
telephone (403) 427-1786; 427-1771
Excellent displays of minerals
(outstanding), rocks and fossils. Several
full-scale dinosaur skeletons are assembled.
Educational exhibits feature local geology
and natural resources. Another gallery is
devoted to Ice-Age mammals with a
full-scale mammoth on display.

Northern Alberta
Institute of Technology
11762-106 Street
Edmonton, Alberta, T5G 2R1
telephone (403) 471-7400

John Janzen Nature Centre
Adjacent to Fort Edmonton Park just
west of the Quesnell Bridge
telephone (403) 428-7900; 434-7446

■ Lapidary Suppliers

Bedrock Supply Ltd.
9617-63 Avenue
Edmonton, Alberta T6E 0G2
telephone (403) 434-2040

Ghossein Museum of World Rocks
and Gemstones Inc.
10320-102 Avenue
Edmonton, Alberta T5J 4A1
telephone (403) 424-2138

Tysons' Fine Minerals Inc.
(by appointment only)
Edmonton, Alberta
telephone (403) 452-5357

The Rock and Gem Shop
15840-111 Avenue
Edmonton, Alberta T5M 2R8
telephone (403) 452-3704

WRITERS' PROFILES

Laurence Andriashek: after formal training in geography and geology from the University of Alberta, he has pursued a 20-year professional career with the Alberta Research Council focused in the areas of Quaternary geology, soils and environmentally sensitive projects dealing with surficial deposits.

James Burns: a vertebrate paleontologist with a 25-year career in the study of bones. As Curator, Quaternary Paleontology, at the Provincial Museum of Alberta for nine years, he has been pursuing and writing about mammalian zoogeography and the glacial history of Alberta for professional audiences and the general public.

Jack Campbell: a paleobotanist who has devoted much of his professional career to the study of coal deposits in Alberta while on the staff of the Alberta Research Council; for more than a decade he headed the Alberta Coal Survey. Now retired, he is acting as a geoscience consultant to industry.

David Cruden: a geologist with special interests in landslides, and who has held a joint appointment in the Departments of Geology and Civil Engineering at the University of Alberta since 1971. He has co-authored a textbook on terrain analysis with Stanley Thomson.

Dixon Edwards: a geologist with 17 years of resource evaluation with the Alberta Research Council has a wide and expert field knowledge of the geology of granular construction materials in Alberta. Special interests include educational geology.

Robert Folinsbee: a geologist specializing in economic geology with broadly based interests extending into many fields including the study of meteorite falls. He has a long and distinguished career in teaching and research at the University of Alberta and is a Fellow of Royal Society of Canada. This former head of the Department of Geology is now Professor Emeritus.

John D. Godfrey: a geologist whose long career spans teaching at the University of Alberta, overseas service at the University of Ceylon and a research program in the study of the Precambrian Shield at the Alberta Research Council. He currently develops and conducts educational travel tours through Godfrey Tours Ltd.

Wylie Hamilton: from an engineering background he has spent the greater part of his career in the practice of geology. Initially with industry, the past 26 years with the Alberta Research Council have seen a strong focus on the geology of industrial minerals of Alberta.

Roger Morton: a geologist specializing in economic geology. Twenty five years teaching at the University of Alberta combined with experience gained from consulting projects and overseas government service provides a broad and varied base in both practical and theoretical aspects of geology. He is a founder-director of Golden Star Resources Ltd., a major Canadian mining corporation operating in Guyana and Suriname.

Ronald Mussieux: graduation in geology and education took him to the Provincial Museum of Alberta where he has been responsible for collecting, cataloging, and preparing exhibits for the general public. His position as Curator of Geology is backed by 20 years of work experience.

Steve Pawluk: a soil scientist with special interests in the genesis and classification of Alberta soils. After a long career in research and teaching, this former head of the Department of Soil Science has recently returned to a full-time research and teaching role at the University of Alberta.

Don Scafe: a formally trained oceanographer with specialization in clay mineralogy. He is largely responsible for extensive research on the clay resources of Alberta as a 25-year staff member of the Alberta Research Council.

John Shaw: a physical geographer with research interests in geomorphology and sedimentology. His professional career has been linked with university appointments and is currently Chair of the Department of Geography at the University of Alberta.

Richard Stein: formally qualified in the fields of geology and hydrogeology. He has practiced hydrogeology for 26 years with the Alberta Research Council and is recognized as a leading authority in this field in Alberta.

Stanley Thomson: a civil engineer with a particular interest in geology. Over a long teaching and research career with the University of Alberta he has keenly pursued and applied geotechnical engineering to the study of slope stability, foundations and tunnelling. He was appointed Professor Emeritus in 1984 and remains active in the geotechnical field.

Milton Wright: trained in anthropology, and specializing in archaeology, with particular application to the prehistory of North America. Field studies in the past 20 years have encompassed most regions of Canada. At the Provincial Museum of Alberta he is involved with collections acquisition, exhibit preparation, public interpretation and culture-resource management.

INDEX